THE COUNCILLOR

THE COUNCILLOR

TWELFTH EDITION

Paul Clayden, M.A. (Oxon.)
Solicitor

A Handy Guide to the
Functions of Councillors

Shaw & Sons

Published by
Shaw & Sons Limited
Shaway House
21 Bourne Park
Bourne Road
Crayford
Kent DA1 4BZ

© Shaw & Sons Limited 2002

First to Eighth Editions .... 1950 to 1970
(by A. Norman Schofield, C.B.E., LL.M., Solicitor)
Ninth Edition 1979
Tenth Edition 1987
Eleventh Edition 1997
(by John Prophet, M.A. (Cantab.), Barrister)
Twelfth Edition 2002

ISBN 0 7219 0853 5

A CIP catalogue record for this book is available
from the British Library

Printed in Great Britain by
Creative Print and Design (Wales), Ebbw Vale

CONTENTS

6 *Contents*

8 *Contents*

PREFACE

This book has been designed to help a councillor in the appreciation of the working of the council and to give an outline of the functions and affairs of the local authority to which he has been elected or co-opted.

There is included a summary of the relations between central and local government, showing how control is exercised over the activities of local authorities. The relationship between central and local government has undergone significant change since the previous edition of this book, largely as a result of the election of a Labour administration in the general election of 1997. The main changes have been: (1) the replacement of compulsory competitive tendering (CCT) by a duty to secure "best value"; (2) the replacement of council tax capping with a more flexible system of council tax limitation; (3) the development of different types of executive arrangements; (4) the promulgation of a new ethical code of conduct for councillors and for council employees; (5) the establishment of a National Assembly for Wales to which most of the powers of the Secretary of State for Wales relating to local government have been devolved; and (6) the establishment of a Greater London Authority with a Mayor directly elected by the electors of Greater London. Changes to the electoral system have also been made.

Certain phrases used in the book are defined as follows:—

"Secretary of State" means the Secretary of State for Transport, Local Government and the Regions in the case of England and the National Assembly for Wales in the case of Wales.

"Principal authority" and "principal council" mean a district, unitary or county council in England and a county or a county borough council in Wales.

"Local council" means a parish or a town council in England and a community or a town council in Wales.

"Local authority" means a principal authority or council and a local council.

Acts of Parliament are referred to as follows:—

LGA 1972   Local Government Act 1972
LGA 1999   Local Government Act 1999
LGA 2000   Local Government Act 2000
LGHA 1989 Local Government and Housing Act 1989

Crown Copyright legislation is reproduced under the terms of Crown Copyright Policy Guidance issued by Her Majesty's Stationery Office.

One of the difficulties which the writers of books on local government face is that both the law and practice change frequently. As a result, a newly published book may be partly out of date almost as soon as it appears. In relation to this book, it has been possible to cover the changes made by the Local Government Acts 1999 and 2000. However, in the autumn of 2000, the government published a Green Paper on the financing of local government which, if enacted, would make major changes to the financial regime of local authorities. Hitherto, no firm legislative proposals have been published.

In October 2001, the government published

proposals for changes to the allowances payable to councillors and co-opted members of local authorities in England. These are summarised in Appendix F. No similar proposals for Wales have yet been published.

In December 2001, a White Paper entitled *Strong Local Leadership; Quality Public Services* was published. This applies only to England. A summary will also be found in Appendix F.

Although the basic law relating to local government is the same in England and Wales, the devolution to the National Assembly for Wales of the powers formerly exercised by the Secretary of State for Wales has led, and will continue to lead, to a divergence between the two countries on matters of detail. This is shown by the enactment of separate codes of conduct (see Chapter 11 and Appendix A) which are effectively identical but which differ in small ways. The relevant statutory instruments reproduced in the Appendices are those for England, but the names and numbers of their Welsh equivalents are given.

Readers will note that councillors, officers and others are referred to in the male gender. This is done purely for convenience and is not intended to detract in any way from the status of female councillors and officers. I am not alone in this practice; it is also adopted by the draftsmen of Acts of Parliament, no doubt because the English language has no single pronoun which applies to people of both sexes.

Paul Clayden

Chapter 1

STRUCTURE OF LOCAL GOVERNMENT IN ENGLAND AND WALES

Historical background

Historically, local government in England and Wales is a fascinating subject and from its study it will be found that local government, whilst not quite as we know it today, existed for centuries before the first Parliament was ever convened. In fact some of our more ancient cities and boroughs have Charters still in existence granted in Saxon times giving to local areas powers which were in effect autonomous government.[1] Indeed, the only method of granting local government to a locality until the early part of the nineteenth century was by a Royal Charter and grants of franchise to corporate bodies and to individuals.

All this was swept away by a new principle which was introduced in the early part of the nineteenth century, namely that a local authority could not carry out any function unless strictly authorised by statute. Parliament as the law-making body does not take part in the local administration of its laws. Indeed, it is one of the features of our constitution that the legislature and the administration are separate. Thus throughout the history of local government, units of local administration were formed to carry out administration in localities. These were, in the main, the counties.

---

[1]   e.g. City of Ripon Charter dated 886 A.D.

In early times the Shire Reeve, or Sheriff, was responsible to the Crown for the administration of the county. Later, Justices of the Peace were appointed and as time passed they were given administrative as well as judicial duties to perform. These Justices of the Peace were forerunners of our present county councils. The Justices sat in session quarterly and these "Quarter Sessions" dealt with both judicial and administrative matters. On the formation of county councils in 1888, the administrative functions of Quarter Sessions passed to the county councils leaving only the judicial functions of Quarter Sessions to the Justices. There are, however, traces still remaining of administrative functions, e.g. Justices still have powers relating to the diversion of highways and footpaths, and in respect of nuisances.

Apart from the counties, a number of urban areas had grown up and many of these had been granted Charters of Incorporation giving them varying powers of local administration. The Municipal Corporations Act 1835 repealed all former constitutions of borough councils and provided a standard formula for the constitution of all municipal corporations, namely a council elected by the burgesses or citizens, aldermen elected by the councillors (the aldermen being one-third of the number of councillors) and a Mayor elected by the aldermen and councillors.

These chartered towns did not cover the whole of the urban areas of the country and in the year 1848 the Public Health Act created Local Boards of Health. The Public Health Act of 1875, which may be regarded as a landmark in the advancement of local administration, gave to these Boards a code of powers in relation to public health and other matters, and established urban and rural sanitary authorities. This was followed by the Local Government Act 1888 which established county councils and county borough councils. By the Local Government Act 1894 the urban and rural sanitary authorities were reconstituted as urban district councils and rural district councils and parish councils were created for rural parishes. That structure was consolidated in the Local Government Act 1933, under which Act it remained the system of local government until the Local Government Act 1972.

While these local authorities were developing in form, other bodies were set up to administer special functions. These included the Turnpike Commissioners, Guardians of the Poor, Education Boards, Highway Boards, Isolation Hospital Boards, Improvement Commissioners, Lighting Commissioners, Burial Boards and other bodies. These were all set up to administer one particular function and, because of this, they are known as *ad hoc* bodies. *"Ad hoc"* is a Latin phrase meaning "to that"; in other words these bodies were appointed to devote their activities "to that" purpose, or for the specific purpose for which they were appointed.

These bodies were popularly elected and responsible direct to the electors. So many bodies doing so many varied local duties created a lack of concerted effort and so Parliament gradually absorbed these boards into the local government machine by transferring their functions one by one to the local authorities. In this way local authorities became the only publicly elected bodies for the area, having accumulated all the powers of *ad hoc* bodies.[1]

---

[1] The Boards of Guardians in 1930 were the last of these bodies to be taken over by local authorities.

In recent years the pendulum has swung back. One after another, the functions of local authorities have been transferred to *ad hoc* boards of a different type from those of the nineteenth century. These functions have been transferred, not to popularly elected boards, but to boards the membership of which is nominated by the Ministers of the Crown. An example of this was the transfer of local authority hospitals. Those hospitals which formerly had been the responsibility of Boards of Guardians and later of the local authorities, together with the development of those hospitals which the local authorities brought about, including maternity hospitals, passed to the State under the National Health Service Act 1946, and are now managed by selected, not elected, authorities.

A further example is the transfer of responsibility for those who need financial support. National Assistance, which followed on Poor Law Relief, has a long history. At first, the parish was responsible for its poor, then came the union of parishes and then the Boards of Guardians followed by the local authorities (county and county borough councils). Now responsibility for social security has largely passed to the State itself, administered by the Civil Service (although local authorities retain responsibility for administering some services, such as community care, housing benefit and council tax benefit). Central administration tends to be heavily bureaucratic and its is interesting to speculate whether the deserving would be better served and the abuses of the modern system better curbed if the administration was returned to more local control.

So today local government is constantly changing its functions. However, there still remains an important field for public administration by locally elected councils. Whilst local authorities are losing certain duties, others are at the same time being added and developed.

Discussion as to whether services are best delivered under the control of locally elected councils now has to embrace complications brought about by changes in the way such services are managed and exercised, albeit that they remain essentially local authority services. For example, local management of schools has been introduced; some authorities have transferred their housing stock to Housing Associations; as a result of compulsory competitive tendering (now replaced by "best value") many services are carried out by private organisations. These changes may at times create difficulties in respect of the acceptance of responsibility for the proper provision of services to the public.

Local government today

The basis of the modern system of local government was created by the Local Government Act 1972 which took effect on 1st April 1974. All the then existing councils, with the exception of parish councils in England, ceased to exist and were replaced by the following:—

(1) Counties

For local government purposes, England (excluding London) was divided into 39 non-metropolitan counties and six metropolitan counties, all with county councils. Most of the non-metropolitan counties retained the well known names, such as Cornwall, Cheshire, Hampshire, Kent and Norfolk, but there were a number of new names, varying from the attractive "Cumbria" to the much disliked "Humberside". The outstanding feature of the new county system, as compared with the one before the 1972 Act took effect, was that the counties absorbed the hitherto independent county boroughs which thereupon ceased to exist, a decision which, in retrospect, some now think was a mistake, since the county boroughs were effective multipurpose authorities (but see the section "Unitary authorities" below).

The six metropolitan counties in the major conurbations, i.e. Greater Manchester, Merseyside, South Yorkshire, Tyne and Wear, West Midlands and West Yorkshire were abolished by the Local Government Act 1985, most of their functions being transferred to the district councils (see below). The Greater London Council was also abolished but has been partially resurrected in the shape of the Greater London Authority (see below).

Wales was then divided into eight counties, i.e. Clwyd, Dyfed, Gwent, Gwynedd, Powys, Mid Glamorgan, South Glamorgan, and West Glamorgan. However, by the Local Government (Wales) Act 1994, all those county councils were abolished as from 1st April 1996 and new unitary principal areas known as counties and county boroughs were established in their place. There are now 11 counties and 9 county boroughs.

(2) Districts

Both the non-metropolitan counties and the metropolitan counties were divided into new districts which completely superseded the former non-county boroughs, urban districts and rural districts. Each new district has a council. A large number of these districts have since applied for and been granted borough status in consequence of which the chairman bears the title of

"Mayor" or sometimes "Lord Mayor". There are fewer districts than under the previous system. In Wales, all districts were abolished as from 1st April 1996 as a consequence of the creation of new unitary principal areas by the Local Government (Wales) Act 1994.

(3) Unitary authorities

As a consequence of the Local Government Act 1992, the Secretary of State is empowered to make orders, following a review by the Local Government Commission for England, for a single authority (sometimes called a unitary authority) to combine all the functions which would otherwise be apportioned between the county and the district. This makes possible, amongst other things, the establishment of authorities in England similar to the old county boroughs. So far, 46 unitary authorities have been established.

(4) Parishes, towns and communities

Before the reorganisation by the 1972 Act, the parish was part of a rural district for local government purposes. Although the rural district councils were swept away, the 1972 Act retained all existing parish councils in England. In addition some non-county borough councils and urban district councils under the previous system were given parish council status by order of the Secretary of State. In Wales, former parish councils became community councils. (Community councils in Wales were largely unaffected by the Local Government (Wales) Act 1994.) Several parish and community councils have given themselves the status of a town council, whereupon the chairman of the parish council has become known as the town Mayor. There are approximately 8,000 parish, town and community councils.

It is an important principle of local government that the smaller councils are independent of, and not subordinate to, the larger councils.

Following the 1972 Act, two permanent Local Government Boundary Commissions were set up – one for England and one for Wales. These Commissions were given extensive powers for reviewing the structure on a continuing basis. For example, the Welsh Commission undertook a Special Community Review to create a proper community structure because the 1972 Act simply designated all the former parishes, boroughs and urban districts as communities irrespective of size and population.

The Local Government Act 1992 replaced the Boundary Commission for England with the Local Government Commission for England with similar but enhanced powers to review the structure, including, if it saw fit, recommending the replacement of two principal authorities in an area by one unitary authority. The provision for the Secretary of State to give directions to the Commission to have regard to any guidance by the Secretary of State was tested in the courts in *R v Secretary of State ex parte Lancashire County Council* [1994] 4 All E.R. 165, when it was held that the Secretary of State had acted unlawfully in giving policy guidelines to the Commission designed to encourage a substantial increase in unitary authorities since it undermined section 13(5) of the 1992 Act which says:—

"Any structural, boundary or electoral change recommended to the Secretary of State under this section shall be such as appears to the Local Government Commission desirable having regard to the need—

(a) to reflect the identities and interests of local communities; and

(b) to secure effective and convenient local government."

From 1st April 2002, the functions of the Local Government Commission for England are transferred to the Electoral Commission (for address, see Appendix E).

Thus the general pattern is that any place in England and Wales (other than some Metropolitan Districts and some unitary authorities) has at least two councils and possibly three, a situation which many consider to be wasteful in terms of administrative costs. It is also confusing to the inhabitants in that it is often difficult to ascertain which council has responsibility for the particular matter which concerns them. People seem to be able to identify easily with the small local council like the parish or town council which represents an identifiable local community such as a village or small town, and also with their traditional county, but where areas have neither an identifiable community nor an historical association, problems can develop. In some cases it is possible for a district to be equated with a large town, but in other cases a desire for districts to be larger has produced curious and often locally resented combinations.

The 1972 Act provided for the principal councils (i.e. the county councils and district councils) to have a number of major functions. However the functions of one council may be transferred to another, and some functions are concurrent. The introduction of the unitary authority simplifies this where such an authority has been established in that the major functions become combined in the one authority. The functions which may be exercised by parish, town and community councils are nearly all concurrent functions with district councils. Which authority exercises them depends on local arrangements.

Where there continues to be a county council and a district council, education (the most expensive local government function) is the responsibility of the county council, but the district council in areas which were formerly governed by metropolitan counties.[1] This applies also to personal social services, youth development and libraries. Planning is divided between county councils and district councils, with the day-to-day administration of planning applications resting mainly with the district councils and the counties looking after strategic planning. Highways (apart from motorways and trunk roads) and transportation are the responsibility of the county councils as highway authorities, with delegation of some functions to district councils under agency arrangements. Consumer protection and waste disposal are the responsibility of county councils, as, too, are police and fire services, although some police and fire services are amalgamated over several counties.

District councils are responsible for housing, most environmental health, refuse collection, clean air, coast protection, markets, local licensing and cemeteries

---

[1]   Although in recent years there has been increasing central control over this function.

(sharing the latter with parish, town and community councils). County and district councils have concurrent powers in respect of museums and art galleries, country parks, conservation areas, rights of way, recreational facilities, local parks, and open spaces, sharing the last four functions with local councils.

London government

Greater London (i.e. the administrative county of London) is governed by the Greater London Authority and 32 London borough councils.

The Greater London Authority (which assumed its powers on 3rd July 2000) consists of the Mayor of London (who is directly elected by the local government electors of London) and the London Assembly, which has 25 members, 14 elected for Assembly constituencies and 11 elected for the whole of Greater London.

The Authority has powers, mainly of a strategic nature, in relation to road, rail and water transport, highways, road traffic, development, police and probation services, fire and emergency planning services, town planning, environmental matters (including biodiversity, waste, air quality and noise) and matters relating to culture, media and sport.

The London boroughs are multipurpose authorities whose functions are broadly equivalent to unitary authorities outside London. They are governed by a Mayor and councillors.

The City of London has a completely separate constitution and is governed by a Lord Mayor, Aldermen and a Common Council.

Cities

Cities have been created in the past by Royal Charter and by common usage.

It was at one period customary, where a town was the centre of the see of a bishop and where in consequence there was a cathedral, to classify the town as a city. Sometimes there were charters, sometimes not.

It is curious that the title of the City of Ripon was confirmed by statute in 1865. Another curiosity is that three parishes are cities – Ely, Ripon and Wells.

Whatever may have been the justification for the title of "city" in the past, such honour is now only conferred by Royal Charter. Towns with populations of less than 200,000 are unlikely to receive such a charter although Cambridge, on account of its standing as a university town, received city status by Royal Charter on the 21st March 1951.

City status adds no additional powers. The Mayor does not automatically become Lord Mayor for that is the subject of a further grant from the Crown. A new city does not necessarily have a bishop or a cathedral.

The Mayor is known by courtesy as "The Right Worshipful the Mayor".

CHAPTER 2

RELATIONS OF LOCAL GOVERNMENT AUTHORITIES WITH CENTRAL GOVERNMENT

Parliament controls by statute the powers of local authorities

During the nineteenth century a new principle evolved. Instead of local authorities having the inherent right, or what in England is called the common law right, to conduct their affairs as they wished, it became established that local authorities could only do those things which Parliament had authorised them to do. Indeed, all that remains today of the old inherent rights is the power to control the method of carrying out the functions which Parliament from time to time gives to the local authorities and the power to make rules as to the conduct of the meetings of the local authority. Parliament has even laid down some rules for controlling these meetings.[1]

Today, the functions of a local authority almost invariably involve the expenditure of money and it is clearly established that a local authority may not spend money unless it has statutory authority to do so. Accordingly, the courts will restrain a local authority from spending public funds on any purpose not authorised by law. For example, many years ago, in an action in the High Court, a Birmingham ratepayer

---

[1]   See Schedule 12 to Local Government Act 1972.

succeeded in preventing the Birmingham City Council from granting free tickets to old age pensioners on the city's transport system because they then had no statutory power to do that.[1] Indeed, in such a lawsuit it is the duty of the local authority to prove that it has the power rather than the person who challenges the action to prove that the local authority has no such power.

The rigidity of this rule has been tempered in recent years by the introduction of the statutory right for any council to spend up to a specified limit on any matter which the council itself considers is in the interests of, and will bring direct benefit to, their area or part of the area, or all or some of the inhabitants.

This rule continues to apply to local councils (in England the current limit is £3.50 per elector per year and in Wales £5 per elector per year). For principal councils, the rule has been relaxed to a greater extent. Subject to some controls and conditions, they may do anything which they consider will assist the promotion or improvement of (a) the economic well-being of their area, (b) the social well-being of their area or (c) the environmental well-being of their area.

The system of government in Britain gives the central government considerable (though not unlimited) powers of ensuring the passage of statutes through Parliament, and consequently thereby controlling local government. These controls are mainly financial. Other methods of control, once considerable, such as the power to control the appointment and removal of principal officials, were

---

[1] *Birmingham Corporation v Prescott* [1954] 3 All E.R. 698. The necessary powers were later granted by statute.

largely removed by the Local Government Act 1972, with further moves in the same direction in the Local Government, Planning and Land Act 1980.

The controls now remaining may be summarised as follows:—

(i)   control of capital expenditure and borrowing;

(ii) control of the amount of government grants and principal authority revenue expenditure. This is in practice the most important and most powerful form of control;

(iii) control by general supervision, e.g. reports, returns, requests for information, schemes, directions;

(iv) control of local legislation, e.g. confirmation of bye-laws;

(v)   control and fixing maximum allowances, e.g. for travelling and subsistence (see Chapter 12, *post*).

Central government's control of capital expenditure

The system of regulating and controlling the capital expenditure and borrowing of principal authorities is set out in Part IV of the Local Government and Housing Act 1989.

Capital expenditure includes expenditure on:—

(i)   the acquisition, reclamation, enhancement or laying out of land;

(ii) the acquisition, construction, preparation, enhancement or replacement of roads, buildings and other structures;

(iii) the acquisition, installation or replacement of plant, machinery and apparatus, vehicles and vessels;

(iv) the making of advances, grants or other financial assistance to any person or body in respect of items (i) to (iii) above;

(v) the acquisition of share capital in any corporate body.

A principal authority may borrow money for any of its functions, but its total borrowing must not exceed its aggregate credit limit. Before the beginning of each financial year the Secretary of State determines his "credit approval" for each principal authority. In this way, the central government keeps a tight grip on overall local authority capital expenditure. The Secretary of State also exercises control over the use by a local authority of capital receipts from the disposal of capital assets.

There is no detailed control by central government over capital expenditure by local councils. The Secretary of State annually gives a general consent to use capital moneys (e.g. arising from the sale of land) for the repayment of debt or for some other capital purpose. He also controls the amount of money borrowed by local councils by making a block allocation for all local councils (there are separate allocations for England and Wales). The amount allocated is administered in England by the National Association of Local Councils and in Wales by the National Assembly (for addresses, see Appendix E).

Central government's control of revenue expenditure

The procedure is that the Secretary of State prepares a report each year on the financing of local government which is presented to and approved by Parliament. The report specifies the basis of distribution of the general grant (the Revenue Support Grant) which the government makes to principal authorities. The aim of the RSG is to allow principal authorities to provide a standard level of service for a standard level of council tax.

The basis for distribution of the RSG is the Standard Spending Assessment (SSA), a complicated set of formulae which aims to recognise variations in the cost of providing services, adjusted to reflect the fact that the revenues of principal authorities from the council tax vary and that they receive a share of the business rates. In practice, there are considerable variations in the level of spending by individual authorities, depending partly upon the policies and priorities of those authorities and partly on factors beyond their control (e.g. sparse population; differences in prices, rents and pay levels in different parts of the country).

The RSG represents more than 90% of government grant to principal authorities. The balance is made up by specific grants for specific purposes. An authority's general grant can be spent on any lawful purpose.

Local councils do not receive RSG.

It can be argued that, with the government funding such a large proportion of local government expenditure from general taxation, considerable central control over local government finances is inevitable and reasonable. It can also be said not to be unreasonable that controls are necessary in order to achieve, as far as possible, a standard level of service throughout the country.

After a period of fairly strict control, the reins of central government have been loosened to some degree. The government has scaled back its powers to restrict council tax increases so that they will be used, if at all, only as a last resort. The requirement for principal authorities (and a few local councils) to submit most of their services to compulsory competitive tendering has been repealed. Authorities are now required to adopt strategies which produce "best value" (see below, page 33).

The government has also signed the Council of Europe's Charter of Local Self Government, to which most governments in Western Europe have also subscribed. Paragraph 1 of Article 3 of the Charter reads as follows:—

"Local self-government denotes the right and the ability of local authorities, within the limits of the law, to regulate and manage a substantial share of public affairs under their own responsibility and in the interests of the local population."

Local government revenue

Local authorities derive their revenue from four main sources:—

1. Income from services provided, and from property owned, by the local authority.

2. The council tax.

3. Government grants.

4. Business Rates.

The first is self-explanatory; charges for recreational services are an example. The third, government grants, have already been discussed.

The fourth relates to the rates paid by businesses. These are set nationally by the government but are collected by district and unitary authorities. The proceeds of the business rate are distributed to principal authorities on a *per capita* basis, i.e. the amount received by each authority is determined by the population of its area.

The proportion of revenue relating to each of the above sources was, in 1998/99, as follows: 1. Income from services, etc., 11%; 2. Council tax, 22%; 3. Government grants, 45%; 4. Business rates, 22%.

Council tax

The council tax (which replaced the unlamented community charge in 1993) is a property-based tax, with properties valued in eight broad bands. The amount of tax payable depends upon the band into which the property falls. The tax is levied only on domestic properties. The amount of the tax is determined in accordance with complicated rules prescribed in legislation and by the Secretary of State.

The Audit Commission

Another system of check upon the finances of local authorities is by means of an audit of the accounts of the local authority. This check is carried out by the Audit Commission, usually on an annual basis. Although the

Audit Commission is an emanation of the State, it endeavours to operate independently of direct central government control.

The duty of the auditor is to see that the accounts have been prepared in accordance with the legal requirements and to see that proper accounting practices have been observed. In addition he has a duty to consider whether, in the public interest, he should make a report on any matter arising out of, or in connection with, the accounts, in order that the matter should be considered by the council or brought to public attention. If he makes such a report, he must send a copy to the Audit Commission.

An auditor has no power himself to decide that a council has acted outside its powers unless it appears to him that an item of account is contrary to law (e.g. an item of unlawful expenditure). In such a case, he may apply to the court for a declaration to that effect. The court may make the declaration and, if it does so, may also order rectification of the relevant accounts. The court no longer has power to order the person responsible for unlawful expenditure to repay it to the council.

The auditor has a new power, introduced by the LGA 2000, to issue advisory notices to warn councils not to undertake unlawful or loss-making activities. When a council receives such a notice, it must itself give notice to the auditor if it intends to continue the course of action about which it has been warned. Clearly, it will only do so if it has received professional legal advice that the course of action is lawful (and, by necessary implication, that the auditor is wrong). The advisory notice procedure replaces the former power of the auditor to issue prohibition notices to control allegedly unlawful activity by local authorities.

In addition to the traditional regulatory audit, the Audit Commission also has an important role to play in examining in more general terms the methods and procedures by which local authorities operate, and thereby check their efficiency, effectiveness and economy of operation.

Central government's control by general supervision

The LGA 1999 has laid a general duty on principal authorities (and a few of the largest local councils: those with a budgeted annual income of £500,000 or more in England or £1,000,000 in Wales) to conduct their affairs in such a way as to secure continuous improvement in the way their functions are exercised, having regard to a combination of economy, efficiency and effectiveness. The duty is called "best value" and involves compliance with a large number of rules and guidelines, the details of which are beyond the scope of this book. This is a form of indirect control over the freedom of authorities to conduct their business as they see fit and it replaces the former compulsory duty to put most services out to competitive tender. In practice, the attainment of "best value" may necessitate seeking competitive tenders for some, or even most, council services.

Indirect control may also be exercised by central government, (a) by requiring local authorities to produce reports, returns and information, (b) by giving directions (e.g. on the handling of certain types of planning application), and (c) by issuing circulars of general guidance or advice which authorities are normally expected to follow.

Central government's control of local legislation

As already stated, a local authority derives its powers from statutory authority. The statutes from which it derives its powers are either public statutes or private statutes. Public statutes are the will of Parliament for the whole country and apply to local authorities of each class alike, whereas private statutes apply to the individual local authority which obtains the private statute from Parliament.

To obtain such a private statute it is necessary for a principal authority to promote a Bill in Parliament and this must be done in accordance with the rules laid down by Parliament. These provide, amongst other things, for public notice in the press of the detailed contents of the Bill. The powers obtained under a principal authority's private Act are generally known as "local Act powers". (Local councils do not have power to promote Bills in Parliament, but may oppose them.)

Parliament has now recognised that local authorities should be left to judge for themselves what local legislation is desirable, but in a tidying-up process all powers under local Acts in force on 1st April 1974 which were not preserved by subsequent general or local legislation automatically expired at the end of 1984.

There is also a system of creating local laws known as bye-laws. These apply to the area of the local authority which makes them and relate to the conduct of people within the area of the local authority. The power to make bye-laws must be contained in an Act of Parliament. Bye-laws made by a local authority are not in force until they have been confirmed by the Secretary of State. This means that in practice the local authority first takes steps to ensure that the bye-laws which they propose to make will receive approval before making them. However, even if they are approved, the validity of bye-laws may be challenged in the courts.

In most cases, the appropriate government departments issue model forms of these bye-laws and tend to oppose any major departure from these standard forms.

State action to prevent illegal and unauthorised acts by local authorities

Apart from the grants to local authorities over which the central government exercises control and other controls provided by legislation, the central government is in no stronger a position to take action against a local authority than an individual citizen: both have the same right to go to the courts to prevent illegal expenditure by "relator action" at the instance of the Attorney-General of the Crown. He will take action in the courts equally for the State as for the individual against any local authority acting "*ultra vires*", that is, beyond its powers.

The Attorney-General may proceed in the High Court for an order to prevent a local authority carrying out its intended unlawful act. Such an order can be obtained swiftly if necessary and can be operative within 24 hours of the local authority's decision. This order may be obtained whether the courts are sitting or not, if a "*prima facie*" case is made out to a judge of the High Court.

It is very rare for the Attorney-General to seek an injunction against a local authority by means of a relator action. Most cases seeking judicial review of the decisions of local authorities are taken by private individuals or corporate bodies seeking a remedy for an alleged injustice. With the coming into force of the Human Rights Act 1998 in October 2000, it is possible that the number of cases involving local authorities will rise. The Local Government Association (for address, see Appendix E) has published advice to member councils.

The local "ombudsman"

A further control on local authorities is carried out by the local ombudsman (see Chapter 9).

Standards Board

Part III of the LGA 2000 has established a Standards Board for England. Its principal function is to deal with allegations that councillors (and former councillors) have failed to comply with their local authority's code of conduct.

In Wales, the same functions are carried out by the local ombudsman.

Chapter 11 *post* discusses the role of the Board.

The relationship of agency between the central government and local authorities

In England and Wales this system has not been developed as much as in other countries. The tendency has been to place the responsibility of administering public services on local authorities, the central government being in the background the whole time to ensure uniformity in the standard of service. To some extent this tendency has been weakened by the establishment of the National Assembly for Wales (for address, etc. see Appendix E), to which central government has devolved many of its functions in Wales, including functions relating to local government.

However, certain functions are administered by principal authorities as agents for the central government when the cost is wholly reimbursed, e.g. the cost of Rent Officers.

The council of every district, unitary and London borough must appoint an electoral registration officer, who is responsible to the central government for the preparation of the register of electors. In this respect these officers are the servants of the Crown and as such are disqualified for election to Parliament.

The manner in which the register of electors is compiled is laid down by Parliament in certain Rules and the electoral registration officer must observe those Rules without any variation suggested by the council.

Chapter 3

ELECTION OF A COUNCILLOR

On deciding to become a candidate for election to a local government body, an individual must ensure that he is qualified to be a candidate. To do this he must assure himself that, on the day he is nominated as a candidate, he is 21 years of age or over, a Commonwealth citizen (which includes a British subject) or a citizen of the Irish Republic or a citizen of a member state of the European Union and either that his name is on the register of electors in the local government area for which he intends to stand as a candidate, or that he has resided in the area (or, in the case of a parish or community, within three miles of the area) for a period of one year, or that he has occupied as owner or tenant land in the area for one year, or that his principal or only place of work has been in the area for one year.

It may be noted that there are also specific *disqualifications* for holding the office of councillor. These are set out in Chapter 13 *post*.

The candidate must be nominated in accordance with rules governing the election of councillors to county and district councils, and of parish and community councillors. These are respectively the Local Elections (Principal Areas) Rules 1986 (as amended) and the Local Elections (Parishes and Communities) Rules 1986 (as amended). The rules apply the rules for parliamentary elections contained in Schedule 1 of the Representation of the People Act 1983, subject to such variations as are appropriate for local elections. Here are set out for the benefit of a person intending to become a candidate a few of the many matters which must be complied with in order that the candidature shall be declared valid by the returning officer.

1. The candidate must be proposed and seconded and, after being proposed and seconded, he must obtain the signatures of eight assentors, except in the case of a parish, town or community council election where assentors are not required.

2. In the nomination paper the candidate must set out his surname and other names in full and his home address. He may, if he so wishes, include a description up to a maximum of six words, which may include a reference to his political or other associations.

3. When obtaining signatures to the nomination paper, the candidate must obtain the signatures of the proposer and seconder first.

4. Great care should be exercised by the candidate in seeing that those who sign the nomination paper are electors for the electoral area. Indeed it is necessary to state after their names the electoral number including the electoral letter of each of the persons signing the paper. A mistake in any of those numbers will invalidate the nomination paper. Their signatures should be their normal signatures.

5. The candidate must also give his consent to nomination and, at the same time that he gives his consent in writing, he must state his qualifications to be a candidate.

A candidate who is new to this kind of thing may ask the chief executive or clerk of the local authority to prepare a nomination paper for signatures. This does not mean that the officer must obtain the signatures of the proposer, seconder, etc. but the officer is always willing to give assistance and advise candidates as to the correct completion of nomination papers.

Nomination papers should always be lodged as far in advance of the closing date as possible since this enables any errors to be rectified and the papers properly resubmitted before the relevant deadline.

The candidate should obtain a free copy of the register of electors from the electoral registration officer for he is entitled to this by statute. This will enable him to check up the electors' signatures, numbers and polling district letters on the nomination paper. In practice, however, in the principal local authorities the political party organisations will oversee this process and manage their candidates' election campaigns.

After nomination the candidate is entitled to be present at the issue of postal ballot papers, to visit the polling stations, and the candidate, the candidate's spouse (if any) and (except in parish or community elections) the candidate's election agent are entitled to be present at the count together with a number of counting agents. A candidate is entitled to seek a recount in the event of a close vote. After being elected, it is customary for a successful candidate to move a vote of thanks to the returning officer and his staff for their work in connection with the election, and this is usually seconded by an unsuccessful candidate. This small act of courtesy is always appreciated.

A candidate's election expenses must not exceed the maximum permitted amount, and he and, where appropriate, his election agent must make a return of them and declaration in the prescribed form within due time, otherwise his membership of the council will be in jeopardy.

Declaration of acceptance of office

The election of a councillor is the principal step towards taking an active part in the affairs of the council, but a second step is necessary. Before he can act in the office of councillor, he is required by statute to make the declaration of acceptance of office.

If this declaration is not made within two months of the day of election and delivered to the chief executive of the council within that two months, then the office automatically becomes vacant at the expiration of the two months. The local authority must then declare the office vacant and signify the vacancy by notice signed by the proper officer of the authority and affixed to the offices of the authority. The local authority has no discretion in the matter. In the case of a local councillor, the declaration must be made before or at the first meeting of the council after his election or, if at that meeting the council so permits, before or at a later meeting fixed by the council.

The declaration must be in the form prescribed by the Secretary of State and can be obtained from the chief executive of the authority.

For the purpose of avoiding disqualification under this provision, the chief executive of the authority will usually prepare the form in readiness so that the councillor may make the declaration as required as soon as he is elected.

Time off for public duties

Under section 50 of the Employment Rights Act 1996, an employer must permit an employee who is a councillor to take time off during working hours for the purpose of performing his duties as a councillor. The amount of time off must be reasonable having regard to the councillor's responsibilities on the council, the circumstances of the employer's business and the effect on that business of the employee's absence. A councillor denied such time off may have the matter determined by an employment tribunal.

Party politics

Virtually all principal authority councillors (and a significant number of local councillors) are elected as members of political parties. The overwhelming majority of principal councils are controlled by one of the main political parties or by some coalition of political parties.

It has hitherto been the general practice for the largest political party, or a coalition of parties, to form a majority group which controls the council. The next largest party, or coalition, forms the opposition. The leader of the majority group is usually called the "leader of the council" and the leader of the largest minority party or group is called the "leader of the opposition". Sometimes the council's Standing Orders recognise the position of leader, and the leaders of the council and of the opposition may have *ex officio* membership of committees and sub-committees. The chairman of the council, or Mayor, usually plays a non-party role during his term of office. The system of party whips, used by the political parties in Parliament, is also widespread among principal authorities. The whips' job is not just to enforce party discipline but, by operating what is referred to in Parliamentary jargon as "the usual channels", can assist the smooth running of the authority by, for example, effecting agreements on nominations to committees or outside bodies.

Where party groups exist, they meet on a regular basis to make policy decisions. The policy decisions of majority parties usually become council decisions in due course, when voted upon at council and committee meetings. However, minority parties must be represented on most committees in proportion to the number of councillors they have on the council: see Chapter 5 *post*.

The system briefly described above will be profoundly affected by the major changes in the way most principal authorities are organised and run which have been enacted by the LGA 2000. These changes are described in Chapter 4.

LOCAL GOVERNMENT EXECUTIVES

Introduction

The LGA 2000 has made radical changes to the ways in which principal authorities in both England and Wales (including London borough councils) perform their functions. (The Greater London Authority is covered by its own legislation, the Greater London Authority Act 1999.) The familiar and long-established system whereby the councillors direct the affairs of the council through the council itself and through committees and sub-committees of the council will, in most cases, be superseded by one or other of the following alternative arrangements:

a. An elected Mayor and two or more councillors appointed to the executive by the Mayor (known as a "Mayor and cabinet executive").

b. A councillor elected as leader of the executive by the authority (an "executive leader") and two or more councillors appointed to the executive either by the executive leader or by the authority (known as a "leader and cabinet executive").

c. An elected Mayor and an officer of the authority appointed to the executive by the authority (known as a "Mayor and council manager executive").

d. A form of executive prescribed in regulations by the Secretary of State. The regulations may, in particular, provide for:—

i.   a form of executive of which some or all of the members are directly elected by the local electors to specified posts;

ii.   a form of executive of which some or all of the members are elected by those electors, but to any specified post;

iii.   a system of voting for use under i. or ii. (e.g. some form of proportional representation).

Various sets of regulations have been made by the Secretary of State making detailed provision for executive arrangements. The principle regulations are listed in Appendix C.

The Mayor is directly elected by the local government electors for the area of the authority. If there are more than two candidates, the election will be conducted under a supplementary vote system (i.e. by proportional representation).

In cases a. and c. above, the arrangements can only be implemented if approved by the local government electors of the area in a referendum (see *post*, page 46). In the case of d. above, a referendum must be held if the relevant regulations so require.

In the case of a district where there is a county council, the Secretary of State may permit other arrangements, including retention of the present system, provided that the population of the district on 30th June 1999 was less than 85,000.

The Secretary of State retains a reserve power to specify alternative arrangements, not requiring the creation and operation of an executive.

Referendums

Every principal authority must draw up proposals for the operation of executive arrangements, having first consulted local government electors and other interested persons in the authority's area. Where the proposals involve the establishment of a Mayor and cabinet executive, or a Mayor and council manager executive, or a prescribed form of executive for which a referendum is required, the authority must:—

(a) hold a referendum before it can implement the proposals; and

(b) draw up an outline of fall-back proposals which it intends to implement if the main proposals are rejected in a referendum. The fall-back proposals must provide for executive arrangements for which a referendum is not required or which are permitted by regulations.

After the initial referendum, a further referendum can be held if at least 5% of the local government electors sign a petition asking for one, but not more frequently than once in five years. The Secretary of State also has a power to direct the holding of a referendum. Detailed provisions about the conduct of referendums are made by regulations under the 2000 Act (see Appendix C).

Principal authority constitutions and guidance

A principal authority which is operating executive arrangements or alternative arrangements must prepare, and keep up to date, its constitution, to be open to public inspection at all reasonable hours and to be on sale at a reasonable price. The constitution must contain:—

(a) information prescribed by the Secretary of State (see Appendix C);

(b) a copy of the authority's Standing Orders (see Chapter 6);

(c) a copy of the authority's code of conduct (see Chapter 11);

(d) such other information (if any) as the authority considers appropriate.

In carrying out its responsibilities in relation to executive and alternative arrangements, a principal authority must have regard to guidance issued by the Secretary of State (see Appendix C for more details).

Where a council has adopted executive arrangements, there will be a differentiation between the role and responsibilities of "executive" and "non-executive" councillors. This topic is covered in Chapter 8.

CHAPTER 5

ANNUAL MEETING

Election of chairman or Mayor where the council is not operating executive arrangements

The election of the chairman (or, if the authority is a borough, the Mayor) is an annual event and is likely to occur at the first meeting a newly elected councillor attends after his election. For those principal councils which are not operating executive arrangements (as to which see Chapter 4 *ante*), the election of the chairman (or Mayor) and the vice-chairman (or Deputy Mayor) is the first business at the annual meeting.

The same procedure applies to local councils, except that they are not obliged to appoint a vice-chairman (but invariably do so). The chairman and vice-chairman of a town council are entitled to be styled the "Town Mayor" and the "Deputy Town Mayor".

At meetings of local councils, in the absence of the chairman, the vice-chairman (if there is one) automatically takes the chair. If there is no vice-chairman, a temporary chairman must be appointed when the elected chairman is absent.

Election of Mayor in London

As indicated in Chapter 1 (*ante* page 23), the Mayor of London is elected directly by the local government electors in Greater London. The Deputy Mayor is appointed by the Mayor from among the members of the London Assembly. Neither the Mayor nor the Deputy

Mayor presides at meetings of the Assembly. The specific offices of Chair of the Assembly and Deputy Chair of the Assembly have been created to fill the roles usually performed by the chairman and vice-chairman of a principal authority outside London. The Chair and Deputy Chair are appointed by the Assembly and normally hold office for the whole period for which they are elected as members of the Assembly (i.e. four years, this being the period between ordinary Assembly elections).

In London borough councils, the Mayor is elected annually by the council but the Deputy Mayor is appointed by the new Mayor. The Deputy Mayor is not the vice-chairman of the council and does not automatically preside at meetings in the absence of the Mayor; in such circumstances a chairman has to be elected for the meeting in question (but he could be the Deputy Mayor).

Election of chairman or Mayor where the council is operating executive arrangements

Where a principal council is operating executive arrangements, a directly elected Mayor cannot be elected as chairman or vice-chairman; nor can a Deputy Mayor (who is appointed by the Mayor). Similarly, a member of an executive (including the leader of the council elected as leader of the executive) cannot be elected chairman or vice-chairman of the council. Subject to these exceptions, the council will elect its chairman and vice-chairman annually.

Appointment of committees

The appointment of committees is an important matter and the newly-elected councillor, if he has any preferences, should make them known in some form either to his political group or to his acquaintances on the council. So many different methods of appointing committees are in operation that no uniform method can be given here. The newly-elected councillor should make it his duty to find out how committees are appointed; this information will be readily obtained from the chief executive of the authority. In most circumstances, there are now legal requirements as to political balance on committees of principal authorities (see Chapter 6).

A councillor cannot be compelled to serve on a committee if he does not wish to do so.

Many councils at their annual meeting appoint co-opted members to serve on their committees, although other councils leave the selection of co-opted members to the committees themselves. The system of co-opting members of the public to serve on council committees can be a good one, for in this way specialised knowledge, information and service can be recruited to the council's activities.

Appointment of overview and scrutiny committees where the council is operating executive arrangements

The LGA 2000 requires a council which is operating executive arrangements to appoint an overview and scrutiny committee or separate overview and scrutiny committees. These committees are principally responsible for (a) reviewing and scrutinising the decisions and actions of the executive, (b) making reports and recommendations to the council or to the executive about the discharge of its functions by the executive, and (c) making reports and recommendations to the council or to the executive on matters which affect the council's area or its inhabitants. In addition, an overview and scrutiny committee may undertake best value reviews where this is not a function of the executive.

An overview and scrutiny committee may not include any member of the executive. It may include persons who are not members of the council but these persons do not normally have a vote (there are some exceptions where the executive is a local education authority).

An overview and scrutiny committee is subject to the same rules in Part VA of the LGA 1972 about publicity for, and attendance of members of the public at, its meetings as other committees of the council. The rules about political balance (see Chapter 6) also apply.

Area committees

The LGA 2000 empowers the Secretary of State to make provision for the executive of an authority to arrange for any of its functions to be carried out by an area committee of the authority. Such a committee will be able to discharge those functions in an area of the authority not exceeding either two-fifths of the total area of the authority or two-fifths of its estimated population, or both. The membership of an area committee must be drawn from councillors representing wards or electoral divisions which are wholly or partly within the area.

The rules about publicity, etc. in Part VA of the LGA 1972 apply to an area committee.

(Legislation providing for area committees in Wales came into force in April 1996 under the Local Government (Wales) Act 1994. In broad effect, the LGA 2000 extends the system to England.)

CHAPTER 6

PROCEEDINGS OF THE COUNCIL

Introduction

Hitherto, the work of a principal council has been carried out in the main through committees. They are of two kinds: standing committees and all other committees. Standing committees are those which are convened regularly on dates which are fixed by the council. The other committees are convened only when necessary to conduct the special business for which they are appointed.

The members of standing committees are normally appointed at the first meeting after an ordinary election. Councillors appointed to committees usually remain members until their term of office expires (i.e. after four years). Some standing committee members are appointed on an annual basis. Members of *ad hoc* committees usually serve for as long as the committee is in existence.

Larger and medium sized local councils usually appoint standing committee members on an annual basis. Smaller local councils often do not appoint any committees but exercise their functions through the full council.

The introduction of executive arrangements (see Chapter 4) under the LGA 2000 will make significant changes to the conduct of business by a principal council. Many of its functions will be carried out by the executive. The council will be required to appoint one or more overview and scrutiny committees which will have oversight of the executive (see *ante*, page 50). The council will also be required to appoint a standards committee (see Chapter 11). Certain functions are allocated between the council and the executive by law. These are specified in regulations made by the Secretary of State (see Appendix C). The Secretary of State and the Welsh Assembly have also issued detailed guidance to principal councils (see Appendix C).

Local councils are not required to make provision for executive arrangements, nor to establish standards committees.

Functions of the council under executive arrangements

The main functions of the council where executive arrangements are operating are as follows:—

(a) to adopt the new constitution (see Chapter 4) and subsequent revisions to it;

(b) to adopt the council's code of conduct for members (see Chapter 11);

(c) to agree the council's budget and policy framework;

(d) to take decisions in respect of functions which are the responsibility of the executive but which are not in accordance with the budget or policy framework agreed by the council;

(e) to take decisions in respect of functions which are not the responsibility of the executive and which have not been delegated by the council to committees, sub-committees or officers;

(f) to make appointments to committees;

(g) to make appointments to the executive where the executive arrangements in the constitution so provide;

(h) to appoint the council manager (under executive arrangements which involve that form of executive);

(i) to make or confirm the appointment of the chief executive.

Membership of committees

A newly-elected councillor must not expect to be appointed to the most important committees unless he has special qualifications for any committee. For example, an experienced chartered accountant may well seek a place on the finance committee, or a solicitor on the law and parliamentary committee.

No councillor can insist on serving on any particular committee, but equally he cannot be compelled to serve on a committee against his wish. A council may remove any member from a committee at any time.

There are occasions when a councillor should not serve on a committee. For example, a building contractor whose company builds houses for the council should decline to become a member of the housing committee and so avoid innuendos which would otherwise follow. Similarly, estate agents practising in the area should avoid the town planning committee. See further the General Principles and Model Code of Conduct (Chapter 11 and Appendix A, *post*).

There is a great deal to be learnt about committee work and the new councillor must expect to undergo a probationary period on some of the less important committees of the council.

In these days when party politics have entered so fully into local government, nominations to committees invariably come from the political groups of the council and it is at the group meetings that a new member should stake his claim for membership of particular committees of his choice. However, local authorities other than local councils must ensure that a committee does not consist only of members from one political group. The number of seats on a committee for each political group represented on the council should be in proportion to the number of councillors of each group, but subject to the majority of seats on the committee falling to the group holding the majority of membership on the council.

Delegation to committees

In recent years, there has been a growing tendency for principal councils to delegate a great measure of power to committees.[1] This tendency has now been reinforced by the creation of executive arrangements under the 2000 Act (see Chapter 4). In effect, the legislation requires the council to delegate many of its powers to the executive. In addition, the council must establish a committee or committees to oversee and scrutinise the executive and a standards committee (see *ante*, page 50). Subject to these constraints, most councils

---

[1]   An executive committee of one councillor is unlawful. *R v Secretary of State ex parte Hillingdon LBC* [1986] 2 All ER 273.

adopt a policy of partial delegation, so that routine matters are dealt with expeditiously by committees, whilst matters of major importance and controversial issues are referred to the full council for decision.

As well as committees, most councils have many sub-committees, both standing and *ad hoc*. The sub-committees usually have delegated to them responsibility for particular aspects of the remit of a committee. For example, a planning committee may delegate its development control functions on a geographical basis to area sub-committees.

Each member of a committee will be sent an agenda some days before a meeting setting out the items to be discussed at that meeting. A good committee member will attend regularly to follow the sequence of matters at each meeting. He will not talk at the committee meeting unless he has a genuine contribution to make to the discussion. Nothing gives so bad an impression to the other members of the committee and to the officers present than a member who talks without having read his agenda papers, or who has missed an earlier meeting where the matter was fully discussed or who talks for the sake of talking on every subject.

The officers of the council attend the committees for the purpose of giving facts to the committee and of tendering advice arising out of their professional knowledge and experience. If they feel that the committee is erring they have a duty to intervene and point out what they think is the best course.

To hold the view that an officer must only tender advice when it is sought from him is entirely erroneous, for indeed it is his duty to tender advice when he thinks it should be given. For example, the chief executive, clerk or legal adviser would be at fault in allowing a committee to do something which is not authorised by law or which he knows or genuinely suspects to be unlawful.

However an officer's duty is to comply with the instructions which he is given by the democratically elected council, and any personal views which he may hold on the issues of policy cannot be used to thwart those instructions.

Raising matters in committee

Often wrongfully appearing on the agenda of a committee is the item "Any other business". This is an item which should not be used. The Local Government Act 1972 specifically states that the only business which can be transacted is that appearing in the summons convening the meeting. It is important for the chairman of the committee to be firm about this.

There is a very sound reason for this provision. Councillors should know beforehand what they are expected to discuss and a councillor may absent himself if nothing really concerns him on the agenda. Likewise a councillor may leave the committee during its sitting. In such circumstances it is improper to raise what may be an important matter which is not on the agenda sent with the summons. That is why the law provides to the contrary. If a councillor has any matter to bring before a committee he must give notice of it to the appropriate officer of the council. Not only should he do this but in addition he would be wise to discuss the matter with the chairman of the committee and the officer concerned.

However, the chairman of a principal council has the authority under section 100B(4)(b) of the Local Government Act 1972 to allow discussion of an item which is not included on the agenda, on grounds of its urgency. A good chairman will have checked with the officers beforehand or, if necessary, at the meeting before exercising this authority.

A newly-elected councillor may have pledged himself in his election address to fight, say, for more open spaces for his electors. After his election, if he is wise, he will go straight to the appropriate officer and consult him about the matter, for all sorts of considerations will apply: for example, the claims of other departments, town planning restrictions, the expense of the land and the like. Some measure of agreement with the chairman and officers will meet with a much greater chance of success than a bold demand in committee for more open spaces.

It is good practice for a member to give notice at one meeting that he wishes to discuss a certain matter at the next meeting. This enables other members to consider the matter between the meetings and also enables the officers to investigate and report on the matter, if necessary.

Many authorities provide in their Standing Orders for the attendance of councillors at meetings of committees of which they are not members where they have a particular interest in certain matters on the agenda. In such cases, they may be permitted by the committee to speak, but not to vote.

Raising matters in council

With certain specified exceptions, a motion can only be placed before the council by a notice of motion which must be in writing to the chief executive of the council within the time provided for in the Standing Orders.

Questions can, however, be asked at a council meeting in two ways. First by giving notice to the chairman of the appropriate committee. He will then answer them at the council meeting. The second method is by asking the chairman of the committee questions on the report of his committee. *Always* give the chairman of the committee and its chief officer notice of any question to be put at the council meeting. You are much more likely to receive a complete and considered answer if you do this.

Committee reports to council

The work of the committees of the council is always the subject of report to the council in some form, either as a report of what the committee has done under delegated powers or by the submission of the recommendations of the committee for the approval of the council. In the latter case, as has been stated, each member will have the opportunity of making observations on the recommendations and of moving amendments at the council meeting.

It is always a wise procedure for a new and inexperienced councillor to watch the working of committees and council before venturing forward with some important proposals. A lack of knowledge of the mechanics of the council may prejudice the success of a good proposal and will almost certainly jeopardise a political "career".

Admission of the public and the press

The public have a statutory right to be present during council meetings and committee meetings. The press have the right to attend as part of the public. Where a meeting is open to the public, the press must, if they ask, be given a copy of the agenda and any supporting documents. It is usual practice to do this even if they do not ask.

At council and committee meetings the council (or committee) has power to exclude the press and the public in certain circumstances where publicity would be prejudicial to the public interest.

This power should be exercised most sparingly for it must be remembered that the public is entitled to know how the council is handling its affairs. Secrecy breeds suspicion and then confidence goes.

In the case of principal councils, i.e. other than local councils, the circumstances of exclusion are strictly defined as being first, where confidential information would be disclosed to the press and public if they attended, and second, where exempt information would be disclosed to the press and public if they attended. In the second case, a resolution of the council or committee must describe the nature of the exempt information relied upon. The resolution (which could be challenged in the courts) must be carefully worded and reported verbatim in the minutes.

The public cannot be excluded simply on the chairman's ruling. The decision must be taken by the council or the committee as the case may be.

Confidential information is that supplied to the

council by a government department on terms which forbid the disclosure of that information to the public,[1] or information which by statute or court order must not be disclosed to the public.

Exempt information is as follows:—

1. Information relating to a particular employee, former employee or applicant to become an employee of, or a particular office-holder, former office-holder or applicant to become an office-holder under, the authority.

2. Information relating to a particular employee, former employee or applicant to become an employee of, or a particular officer, former officer or applicant to become an officer appointed by, a Magistrates' Court committee or a probation committee.

3. Information relating to any particular occupier or former occupier of, or applicant for, accommodation provided by or at the expense of the authority.

4. Information relating to any particular applicant for, or recipient or former recipient of, any service provided by the authority.

5. Information relating to any particular applicant for, or recipient or former recipient of, any financial assistance provided by the authority.

6. Information relating to the adoption, care, fostering or education of any particular child.

---

[1] A good example of the central government making its own rules about what the public should know.

7. Information relating to the financial or business affairs of any particular person (other than the authority).

8. The amount of any expenditure proposed to be incurred by the authority under any particular contract for the acquisition of property or the supply of goods or services.

9. Any terms proposed or to be proposed by or to the authority in the course of negotiations for a contract for the acquisition or disposal of property or the supply of goods or services.

10. The identity of the authority (as well as of any other person, by virtue of paragraph 7 above) as the person offering any particular tender for a contract for the supply of goods or services.

11. Information relating to any consultations or negotiations, or contemplated consultations or negotiations, in connection with any labour relations matter arising between the authority or a Minister of the Crown and employees of, or office-holders under, the authority.

12. Any instructions to counsel and any opinion of counsel (whether or not in connection with any proceedings) and any advice received, information obtained or action to be taken in connection with:—

    (a) any legal proceedings by or against the authority; or

    (b) the determination of any matter affecting the authority;

(whether, in either case, proceedings have been commenced or are in contemplation).

13. Information which, if disclosed to the public, would reveal that the authority proposes:—

   (a) to give under any enactment a notice under or by virtue of which requirements are imposed on a person; or

   (b) to make an order or direction under any enactment.

14. Any action taken or to be taken in connection with the prevention, investigation or prosecution of crime.

15. The identity of a protected informant.

The above rules apply to sub-committees as well as committees. However, in the case of parish, town and community councils, the statutory right of the public and the press to be present does not at present extend to sub-committees appointed directly by the council.

Public participation

Many councils have adopted measures to encourage public participation. In some cases part of a full council meeting is available for public questions or the submission of petitions. In others, members of the public may be invited to address committees or sub-committees before decisions are reached on topics about which they hold particular views.

Standing Orders

The rules which govern the conduct of the business of the council and its committees, other than those incorporated in legislation, are called Standing Orders. The chief executive of the local authority should always provide each newly-elected councillor with a copy of these which should be studied closely by the new councillor. These Orders will give him the rules for the conduct of debate and committee work. They will tell him the rules for bringing motions before the council, for moving amendments, for raising questions, for length of speeches, rights of reply and the like. A councillor who is a student of Standing Orders is always an asset to the council, but a councillor who is not becomes a burden and a handicap to debate, and frequently a disappointed and frustrated person.

It is one of the privileges of a councillor in a council meeting to see that other members obey Standing Orders. A breach of Standing Orders can be challenged only on "a point of order". This privilege must not be abused by using it for something which is not a point of order.

The council should not agree to Standing Orders being "suspended" except in a real emergency, otherwise the conduct of the council's business may be unnecessarily prolonged and the standard of debate lowered.

As a further example of central government interference in the manner in which local authorities conduct their business, the Secretary of State was empowered by the Local Government and Housing Act 1989 to make regulations requiring local authorities other than local councils to make certain procedural Standing Orders, particularly in respect of reviewing the decisions of committees and sub-committees, and in respect of the manner of voting. The Local Authorities (Standing Orders) Regulations 1993 and the Local Authorities (Standing Orders) (England) Regulations 2001 (see Appendix D) have provisions relating to the appointment of chief officers, disciplinary action against chief officers, the recording of votes in meetings (including committees and sub-committees), and the signing of minutes at extraordinary meetings.

It is not essential for a small local council to have Standing Orders (except in relation to contracts for the supply of goods or materials or for the execution of works), but even then it may be useful to have a "model" set from NALC (for address, see Appendix E) for guidance in case some difficulty on procedure arises.

"Privilege" of councillors at meetings

There is unfortunately a mistaken view held by many councillors that they are free to say anything they like in council meetings for they imagine that the council meeting is a completely privileged occasion.

There is in fact no special protection afforded by the law to members of a council who make defamatory statements at meetings of the council. There are, however, certain defences to an action for defamation, and a member of a council may be able to bring the language he uses within the ambit of one of those defences.

Qualified privilege

Qualified privilege may be claimed if the member of the council making a statement about a person can show that he made it without malice and in pursuit of a public duty. Thus, if a member has a sound reason for believing that some malpractice is occurring in connection with the council's funds, he is under a public duty to inform the council. If the statement he makes is found to be true it will not be defamatory (see 'Justification' below). If it is found not to be true, the member may claim qualified privilege if he acted without malice.

Express malice may defeat a plea of qualified privilege, and in this sense "malice" means, first, personal spite in the contents of the statement or, second, personal spite in the mode or extent of the publication. Mere carelessness will not suffice.

Evidence of malice may be found in the statement itself, i.e. if the words used are excessive and disproportionate to the facts. It may also be inferred from the relations between the parties.

Evidence of malice in the mode of publication is illustrated by wider dissemination of the statement than is necessary, such as shouting for others to overhear, or sending an open postcard instead of a closed letter. Mere dictation to a typist in the normal course of business is not evidence of excessive publication.

The privilege is limited strictly to matters of public concern and the publication must be for the public benefit. So, speaking generally, statements made at meetings of local authorities are thus privileged. This special defence does not extend to anything written or said which is not relevant to the discharge of the duty or the exercise of the right which creates the privilege. If, therefore, a person can prove that the statements or criticisms complained of went beyond reasonable or forceful debate and were defamatory (as, for example, a torrent of defamatory invective), and were influenced by indirect or ulterior motives, he might well be justified in issuing a writ.

Fair comment

Another defence to an action for defamation is that of fair comment.

This defence relies on alleging that the statement is a fair comment on a matter of public interest. Honest criticism is essential and healthy, and is recognised as such by the law. The elementary requisites of fair comment are: first, the matter must be of public interest; second, it must be an expression of opinion based on proved facts; third, the comment must be fair; and last, there must be no malice.

Justification

Justification is another defence. In this defence the defendant may prove the statement to be true. It is a question for the court whether substantial truth is sufficient.

A defence of justification does not fail by reason only that the truth of every charge is not proved, if the words not proved to be true do not materially injure the claimant's reputation having regard to the truth of the remaining charges.

CHAPTER 7

REPRESENTATION ON OTHER BODIES

A great deal of valuable work is done by members of local authorities when serving as representatives of their authorities on outside bodies. The newly-elected councillor will be expected to take his share of this important aspect of the council's work. Thus a councillor may find himself co-opted on to a committee of another local authority, since such a committee may, providing it is not a finance committee, co-opt non-members. Alternatively or in addition, he may be co-opted on to other public or quasi-public bodies, such as health trusts.

Councillors on authorities other than education authorities may be invited to participate at some level in educational administration and, in the case of primary schools, district councils which are not unitary authorities and local councils may have a say in respect of appointing governors.

In almost every town and district in the country there exist charitable funds and there is a growing tendency to invite local government representation upon their management committees. In fact it is frequently the case that the chief executive or clerk of the local authority is also secretary of the charity.

It is important that this representation on outside bodies is fully maintained in the interest of the people whom the councillor represents. It is also important that regular attendance at the meetings of these outside bodies should be maintained in order to preserve continuity of co-operation between the local authority and the outside body.

The newly-elected councillor should welcome the opportunity of serving on these outside bodies for only by so doing can he obtain a full appreciation of the part which these bodies play in local administration and the well-being of the community.

In most cases, allowances to members apply when the councillor attends such outside bodies. The chief executive of the authority will tell the councillor when they apply to him.

CHAPTER 8

RESPONSIBILITIES AND LIMITATIONS OF COUNCILLORS

Election to the office of councillor gives the councillor great responsibilities towards his electors. In a democracy, the elected member is entrusted with duties towards all persons in his constituency irrespective of the fact that they may not have voted for him. In some councils, the pressures of party political control may be very considerable but, even so, he should always bear in mind this overall responsibility.

The councillor should represent the views of his constituents in the council, in the executive (if a member) and in committees and sub-committees. He should also consult them about general policy issues relevant to his area (e.g. best value, community planning) as well as on issues of particular local concern.

This public duty must not be influenced by private and personal interests. The Secretary of State, in agreement with the local authority associations (for addresses, see Appendix E), has promulgated general principles to govern the conduct of elected and co-opted members of "relevant authorities" (which include all types of local authority in England and Wales). He has also specified Model Codes of Conduct for councillors. Both are reproduced in Appendix A. (See also Chapter 11 on declaration of interests.)

A councillor has no right to a roving commission to go and examine books or documents of a council because he is a councillor. Mere curiosity to fish around to inspect documents is not sufficient.[1] However, following some uncertainty on this matter arising from two court decisions in the 1980s, the position has now been restated by statute. Any document which is in the possession or under the control of a principal council and which contains material relating to any business to be transacted at a meeting of the council or at a committee or sub-committee of the council is open to inspection by any member of the council. However, that right is subject to exemptions if the proper officer decides that it discloses confidential information under one of the categories set out on pages 61 to 63 above.

A councillor has a right to inspect the accounts at all reasonable hours. The papers which he receives for council and committee work *are often confidential* and he should not disclose the contents of those papers to outsiders. If he requires information he should approach the chief executive of the council for it. A councillor has no right to require an officer of the council to compile information for him. This can only be done through a committee and then the information will be sent to all members of the committee. He should not seek information from other local authorities except through the chief executive of his own council. If he does attempt to do so he will either receive a negative reply or cause the officer of that other authority to send a copy of the correspondence to the councillor's chief executive.

The chief executive of a local authority is always

---

[1] Taken from the judgment in the case of *R v Southwold Corporation* (1907) 97 LT 431.

anxious to assist members by giving and obtaining for them the fullest information for their work.

The councillor should not visit or inspect any of the buildings or works of the local authority without first obtaining the approval of the council or the appropriate committee. A councillor who visits council properties and establishments without such authority is technically a trespasser. He is advised also to notify the appropriate official of his intentions when he will receive all reasonable assistance towards his visit. **It should always be remembered that the official takes his instructions from the council and its committees only and not from individual councillors**.

Here it would be useful to impress upon the new councillor the relationship between the official and the council. The official is engaged by the council for three main functions, namely Executive, Administrative and Advisory. The council decides the policy but the official carries it out, and the way in which he carries out the instructions of the council is in accordance with his recognised professional skill and knowledge. Unless specifically instructed by the council, a councillor must not take part in the execution of works or actions ordered by the council. He must not write letters on behalf of the council or sign public notices. Those functions are the responsibility and duty of the official. The official's duty is to have in mind the best and most effective and efficient means of carrying out the council's decision.

A councillor's actions may also be limited or curtailed by the party control exercised over him. Where there is a system of control of council matters through caucus groups of members of the council, these groups determine beforehand what line of action shall be taken by the members of those groups when matters come before the council and its committees. The disciplinary control exercised by these groups is usually powerful, for if any member breaks away and acts contrary to the decisions of the group on any important issue he will probably lose the support of his party at the next election.

The advantage of the group system is that it ensures that members of the respective parties put forward clear-cut views at the meetings of the council. The disadvantage is that the individual councillor, if he is a member of such a group, may be required to subordinate what he considers to be in the best interests of his electors to what his group so consider.

Further, the extension of this system might well reach the stage when directives are given from political headquarters as to the line of action which ought to be taken locally. When that time arrives the discretion of the local councillor will be seriously limited, and it is also questionable whether such directives are in any sense democratic.

Executive councillors

Councillors who are members of an executive (see Chapter 4) will have much wider responsibilities than non-executive members. They will be the leaders in preparing the council's budget and setting its general policies. They will be responsible for ensuring that the necessary resources are available to implement the council's policies.

Training and support

Every principal authority will (or should) have a training and support programme for councillors. With the introduction of executive arrangements (see Chapter 4), councillors who are members of an executive will have greater responsibilities than in the past. Councillors who are not executive members will have altered responsibilities, with greater emphasis on their representational role and on holding the executive to account through scrutiny and overview arrangements. Standards committees (see Chapter 11) will have a specific responsibility to provide training and advice about the council's code of conduct.

Local councils do not usually have individual training and support programmes for their members. However, local councillors will benefit from training. The government has announced a national training scheme for local councillors, which will be managed by the Countryside Agency, with input from the Local Government Association, the National Association of Local Councils and the Improvement and Development Agency. The Association of Councillors also runs training courses and programmes for councillors of all types of local authority. (See Chapter 15 for details of the associations and Appendix E for addresses.)

CHAPTER 9

PREVENTION OF CORRUPTION

The integrity of a councillor is extremely important and no councillor should bring his position into disrepute by obtaining any illegal financial gain from his activities as a councillor. All councillors should read carefully the relevant paragraphs of the Model Codes of Conduct (Appendix A).

Two Acts of Parliament deal specifically with the problem of corruption of members of local authorities. The Public Bodies Corrupt Practices Act 1889 creates a two-edged offence, namely the receiving of a bribe and the giving of a bribe. In certain cases a presumption of corruption arises by virtue of the second of these Acts, i.e. the Prevention of Corruption Act 1916.

Although the existence of the statutes indicates certain offences which sometimes creep into public life, it is most gratifying to note that amongst the many tens of thousands of councillors serving voluntarily year by year in this country, a prosecution under the legislation is very rare indeed.

It may be useful to quote that part of the 1889 Act so far as it affects a member of a local authority:—

"Every person who shall by himself or by or in conjunction with any other person, corruptly solicit or receive, for himself, or for any other person, any gift, loan, fee, reward, or advantage whatever as an inducement to, or reward for, or otherwise on account of any member ... of a public body ... doing or forbearing to do anything in respect of any matter or transaction whatsoever, actual or proposed, in which such public body is concerned shall be guilty of a misdemeanour."

In *R v Smith* [1960] 1 All E.R. 256 the Court of Criminal Appeal held that a person acts corruptly if he offers a fee or reward to an officer of a local authority deliberately and with the intention of it being a corrupt inducement even if there was no intention of obtaining any favour to his own advantage.

The 1889 Act imposed a penalty of up to two years' imprisonment, but this was amended by the Prevention of Corruption Act 1916 and the Criminal Justice Act 1988 to a maximum of seven years' imprisonment or a fine, or to both.

In addition to these penalties the amount of any gift, loan, fee or reward obtained may be directed to be paid to the public body. The member is also liable to be adjudged incapable of being elected or appointed to any public office for five years from the date of his conviction and also to forfeit any such office held by him at the time of his conviction.

In the event of a second conviction for a like offence, a member is liable, in addition to the penalties already named, to be adjudged to be forever incapable of holding any public office, and to be incapable for five years of being registered as an elector or voting at a Parliamentary election or an election of members of any public body.

The term "reward" covers receipt of money for a past favour even if there was no prior arrangement or agreement.

CHAPTER 10

THE LOCAL OMBUDSMAN

Under the Local Government Act 1974 (as amended) bodies of commissioners, known as Commissions for Local Administration, have been established for England and Wales (for addresses, see Appendix E). They are responsible for conducting investigations into complaints of maladministration against local authorities, other than local councils. They are commonly referred to as local ombudsmen.

A complaint must be made in writing and must be sent either:—

(a) direct to the appropriate Commissioner; or

(b) to a councillor for the authority concerned, who may forward it to the Commissioner. Alternatively, another councillor of the same authority may do so. If the Commissioner is satisfied that a request to a councillor to forward a complaint has not been acted on, he may act on the complaint directly.

Before investigating a complaint, the Commissioner must be satisfied that the complaint has been brought to the notice of the authority, and that the authority has been given a reasonable opportunity to investigate and reply to it. Many authorities have set up their own procedures to look into complaints and thus may thereby attend to the matter before it is thought necessary for the local ombudsman to be approached. The council's monitoring officer has a duty to report to the council on any matter which he thinks has given, or may give, rise to a complaint.

Maladministration is not defined, but it is usually taken to mean administrative action (or inaction) which has led to unfairness to a member of the public. The Commissioner will not investigate matters where the complainant has a remedy through a court or tribunal.

Following an investigation, the Commissioner will prepare a report and may make recommendations. If the Commissioner finds maladministration and the authority does not remedy it to the satisfaction of the complainant, until recently there appeared to be no way in which the complainant could pursue the matter further. However, the avenue of judicial review to the High Court may in exceptional circumstances be available. Nevertheless, a good deal of responsibility rests on the local authority and the councillors to deal properly and fairly with any complaint, or finding by the Commissioner.

The authority has power to make a payment to, or provide some other benefit for, a person who has been adversely affected by an action by the authority which amounts to, or may amount to, maladministration.

The Commission in Wales also has responsibility for enforcing standards of conduct for councillors, a responsibility exercised in England by the Standards Board (see Chapter 11).

CHAPTER 11

STANDARDS OF CONDUCT AND MEMBERS' INTERESTS

Standards of conduct

It is most important that a councillor should not take advantage of his position and use it for his own personal gain. For this reason, the LGA 2000 gives the Secretary of State powers:—

(a) to specify the principles which govern the conduct of councillors and co-opted members of all local authorities in England and Wales; and

(b) to issue a model code of conduct for councillors.

The powers have been exercised in the Local Authorities (Model Code of Conduct) (England) Order (S.I. 2001 No. 3575) and the Parish Councils (Model Code of Conduct) Order 2001 (S.I. 2001 No. 3576) (for England) and the Conduct of Members (Model Code of Conduct) (Wales) Order 2001 (S.I. 2001 No. 2289) (for Wales). The two sets of regulations are effectively identical. The English Orders are reproduced in Appendix A.

Under Part III of the LGA 2000, every relevant authority (i.e. local authority) is required to adopt its own code of conduct. This must include any mandatory provisions in the model code and may include any optional provisions it contains. In fact, the whole of the model code is mandatory. In addition, the authority may include non-mandatory provisions which are consistent with the model code.

Every councillor and co-opted member must, within two months after the date on which the authority adopts its code of conduct, give the authority a written undertaking to observe the code whilst exercising his functions as a councillor or co-opted member. The form of undertaking is incorporated in the declaration of acceptance of office which a councillor must sign after election (see Chapter 3 *ante*), so that newly elected councillors can give their undertaking as soon as they attain office. Councillors elected before the authority adopts its code of conduct may not act as councillors until they have given their undertaking.

The former National Code of Local Government Conduct has been entirely superseded by the codes of conduct of individual authorities.

Compliance with the code of conduct is monitored by the standards committee which every principal authority is obliged to establish. The composition of standards committees is partly prescribed by the Relevant Authorities (Standards Committees) Regulations 2001 (S.I. 2001 No. 2812), which is reproduced in Appendix A. The functions of the standards committee are:—

(a) to promote and maintain high standards of conduct by councillors and co-opted members of the authority; and

(b) to help councillors and co-opted members to observe the authority's code of conduct.

The standards committee of a principal authority also acts as a standards committee for the local councils within its area (if any).

In England, a national Standards Board has been

established to have general oversight of the conduct of councillors and co-opted members of local authorities. In Wales, this function is performed by the Commission for Local Administration in Wales. (For addresses, see Appendix E.) The Board and the Commission may issue general guidance to local authorities.

It is open to any person to make a written allegation to the Board or the Commission that a councillor or a co-opted member of a local authority has failed, or may have failed, to comply with the authority's code of conduct. The Board and the Commission have extensive powers of investigation, etc. which in England are exercised by ethical standards officers and in Wales by Local Commissioners. The monitoring officer of the authority of which the person under investigation is a councillor or a co-opted member will almost invariably be involved as well. Since local councils do not have monitoring officers, the monitoring officer for the relevant principal authority will have the same powers in relation to allegations against local councillors as he has in relation to those against members of his own authority.

There is an elaborate procedure laid down in the LGA 2000 for the conduct of investigations into allegations that a councillor or co-opted member has failed to comply with the code of conduct, for the production of reports and the reference of cases to adjudication panels and case tribunals. At the end of the day, where a case tribunal rules that a councillor or co-opted member has breached the code of conduct, the tribunal may:—

(a) suspend or partially suspend that person from membership of the authority; or

(b) disqualify that person from being, or becoming, a member of the authority or of any other authority.

Suspension or partial suspension cannot be for longer than one year. Partial suspension involves loss of particular functions and responsibilities as a councillor or co-opted member, but not membership of a committee, sub-committee or joint committee, or membership of an executive. Disqualification cannot be for longer than five years.

There is a right of appeal to the High Court against a ruling by a case tribunal.

Members' interests

The LGA 2000 lays down a new framework for the disclosure and registration of members' interests. The former legislation in sections 94 to 98 of the LGA 1972 and section 19 of the LGHA 1989 has been repealed, so that it is no longer a criminal offence not to declare pecuniary interests or to fail to register relevant interests.

Part 2 of the model codes of conduct (reproduced in Appendix A) deal with members' interests. The possible sanctions for breaching this part of the code are described in the previous section of this chapter: suspension, partial suspension or disqualification.

In most circumstances, a councillor or co-opted member who has a prejudicial interest (defined in paragraph 10 of the model code) in a matter which comes before the council must withdraw from the meeting and, if a member of the executive (see Chapter 4), must not exercise any executive functions in relation to the matter. However, the authority's standards committee has power to grant a dispensation – see paragraph 11 in the model code relating to authorities operating executive arrangements and paragraph 12 of the model code for authorities not operating such arrangements in the Local Authorities (Model Code of Conduct) Order and paragraph 12 of the model code relating to parish councils in the Parish Councils (Model Code of Conduct) Order in Appendix A.

As well as a code of conduct, all principal authorities (and many local councils) will have Standing Orders to regulate the conduct of their business. These will often provide for a councillor or co-opted member to take no part in the discussion of a matter in which he has a declarable interest and to withdraw from the meeting when the matter is debated.

Employment by the council

The law makes clear that a member of a local authority may not be a paid employee of the authority. Section 116 of the LGA 1972 provides as follows:–

"A person shall, so long as he is, and for twelve months after he ceases to be, a member of a local authority, be disqualified for being appointed by that authority to any paid office,[1] other than the office of chairman or vice-chairman."

Section 112(5) of the LGA 1972 provides that a member of a local council may be employed as an officer (usually as clerk) without remuneration.

---

[1] The disqualification applies even if the person appointed to the paid office agrees to work without payment, i.e. in an honorary capacity: *AG v Ulverston UDC* [1944] 1 All ER 475.

The foregoing legislation does not prevent an employee of one authority being a member of another. However, section 1 the LGHA 1989 disqualifies certain senior officers of principal authorities from being members of *any* principal authority, although membership of a local council is not prohibited.

ALLOWANCES TO COUNCILLORS

The system for the payment of allowances to members of principal authorities is authorised by section 18 of the LGHA 1989, as amended by section 99 of the LGA 2000. The details are contained in the Local Authorities (Members' Allowances) Regulations 1991 (as amended) and the Local Authorities (Members' Allowances) Regulations 2001. Both sets of Regulations are reproduced in Appendix B. The system of allowances for members of local councils is different and is covered separately below.

Changes to the current system of allowances have been proposed by the government – see Appendix F.

Members of principal authorities
Basic, special responsibility and childcare and dependent carers' allowances

The 1991 Regulations require principal authorities to make a scheme for the payment of allowances. The scheme provides for the payment of the following:—

(a) a basic allowance for each member which is the same for every member;

(b) a special responsibility allowance for members who undertake additional responsibilities, e.g. chairman and leaders. The amount does not have to be the same and is more likely to reflect the nature of the additional responsibilities and extra work undertaken. Regulation 9 provides for the recognition in the scheme of political groupings;

(c) a childcare and dependent carers' allowance. This is a new allowance, resulting from an amendment to the LGHA 1989 by the LGA 2000, payable to those councillors who incur expenditure for the care of children or dependent relatives whilst undertaking approved duties.

All the above allowances must be declared as income for tax purposes, but any expenses wholly and necessarily incurred in the performance of the duty (and not otherwise reimbursed) may be set off against the allowance.

Travelling and subsistence allowance

A member may claim allowances in respect of expenses incurred for travelling and subsistence on any approved duty (as defined in Regulation 10 of the 1991 Regulations). The amounts are repayment of moneys actually spent and are not therefore subject to tax. The maximum amounts which may be claimed are prescribed by the Secretary of State but authorities may pay less than the maximum. A form for claiming allowances can be obtained from the appropriate officer of the authority. Members should take great care to ensure that their claims correspond exactly with the expenditure incurred. They should obtain, and keep, receipts for all claimed expenditure wherever possible.

Conference and meeting allowance

A member may be paid an allowance for attending conferences or meetings as an approved duty.

Remuneration panel

Under the LGHA 1989, as amended by the LGA 2000, every principal authority is required to establish and maintain an independent remuneration panel. The function of the panel is to make recommendations to the authority about the allowances to be paid to elected members. The recommendations will usually include the level of the basic allowance for all members, the categories of special responsibility for which a special responsibility allowance is to be paid and the levels of the special responsibility and childcare and dependent carers' allowances.

Members of local councils

The method for the payment of councillors as explained above does not apply to local councillors who in general terms are not regarded as persons who should receive payment for carrying out their services. They may however qualify for certain allowances.

Attendance allowance

An attendance allowance is payable if they carry out an approved duty, *but only if it is performed outside the area of the parish or community.* An approved duty is any duty specified in Regulation 16 of the Local Authorities (Members' Allowances) Regulations 1991 (see Appendix B, *post*) or specifically approved as such by the council. The amount payable is such reasonable amount as the council itself determines, subject to an upper limit which is prescribed by the Secretary of State. The position in respect of tax for any such allowance is similar to that indicated above for attendance allowances for councillors of principal councils.

Financial loss allowance

In the case of members of committees of local councils who are not entitled to an attendance allowance because they are not councillors of the authority, there is provision for a payment instead of a financial loss allowance in respect of any loss of earnings necessarily suffered, or additional expense incurred (other than travelling or subsistence expenses) in performing an approved duty outside the area of the parish or community. Such a payment is likewise subject to a maximum prescribed by the Secretary of State. It is, however, not taxable since it relates to actual losses or expenses incurred.

A local councillor may give written notice to his council that he wishes to receive a financial loss allowance instead of an attendance allowance. The notice will take effect one month from the date it is given. The councillor may revert to an attendance allowance by further written notice. A councillor wishing to take advantage of these provisions should consult the financial officer of the council to ensure that the correct procedures are followed.

Attendance at conferences or meetings

An attendance allowance and an allowance for travelling and subsistence may be paid to any local councillor in respect of attendance at any conference or meeting (other than a meeting of the council itself within its area) which the council itself considers relates to the interests of the area (other than one called in respect of a trade or business or which is wholly or partly political).

Travelling and subsistence allowance

As with councillors of principal councils, a member of a local council may obtain repayment of travelling and subsistence expenses in accordance with prescribed rates necessarily incurred in carrying out an approved duty, subject to the definition of an approved duty and the geographical limitations indicated above. These amounts are not subject to tax.

Chapter 13

RESIGNATION AND CEASING TO HOLD THE OFFICE OF COUNCILLOR

Voluntary resignation

A councillor resigns his office by notice in writing signed by him and delivered to the chief executive or clerk of the authority, except in the case of a parish, town or community councillor when it should be addressed to the chairman of the council. The resignation becomes effective on receipt of the resignation by the recipient. There is no statutory procedure for withdrawing such a notice, neither has the resignation to be reported to the council in order to be effective. The purported withdrawal of a resignation is ineffective as the resignation is final when received by the proper officer of the authority or the chairman as the case may be.

Disqualifications for office of councillor

A member of a council ceases to hold that office in the following circumstances.

1. On the normal termination of his period of office.

2. The court may order him to forfeit his office if he is convicted for corruption under the Public Bodies Corrupt Practices Act 1889, and if he is convicted a second time under that Act he may be adjudged incapable forever of holding a public office. Similarly, a member convicted under the Representation of the People Act 1983, under the provisions relating to corrupt

and illegal practices, is incapable of holding office for five years.

3. He may lose his office by failure to attend meetings. The law provides that if a member of a local authority fails throughout a period of six consecutive months to attend any meeting of the local authority he shall, unless the failure was due to some reason approved by the local authority *before* the expiry of that period, cease to be a member of the authority. Approval cannot be given after the six-month period has elapsed. Absence due to service with the Armed Forces during war or any emergency does not cause the office to be lost. The attendance of a member at a meeting of a committee or sub-committee of the local authority is regarded as attendance at a meeting of the authority, but attendance at a meeting of a joint committee, joint board or other body will only count as attendance at a meeting of the authority when any functions of the local authority have been transferred or delegated to that body. Where a member is suspended or partially suspended (see Chapter 10, page 81, *ante*), the period of suspension is disregarded in calculating the six month period.

4. A member who has failed to make the declaration of acceptance of office within the prescribed timescale (see *ante*, page 41) automatically ceases to be a member.

5. A member who is adjudged bankrupt or who has a made a composition or arrangement with his

creditors ceases to be a member. However, the disqualification by reason of bankruptcy is removed and ceases if the adjudication in bankruptcy is annulled, or the bankrupt obtains his discharge. In the case of composition or arrangement, the disqualification is removed on payment of his debts in full, or otherwise on the expiration of five years from the date when the terms of the deed of composition or arrangement are fulfilled.

6. A councillor ceases to be a member if he takes or holds any paid office or employment (other than that of chairman, vice-chairman or deputy chairman), the appointment to which is made by the council or any committee or sub-committee of the council.

7. If within five years before his election or since his election he is convicted of an offence and has passed upon him a sentence of imprisonment (whether suspended or not) for a period of not less than three months without the option of a fine.

8. If he is disqualified from office following a decision by a case tribunal (see Chapter 11, page 81, *ante*). The disqualification runs from the expiry of the period allowed for making an appeal or an application or, if an appeal or application is made, from the date on which the appeal or application is finally disposed of.

CHAPTER 14

OFFICERS OF LOCAL AUTHORITIES

A local government officer is a servant of both the council and the public. Although he is appointed by the council which pays his salary, he has nevertheless duties to the public to see that their rights are protected. He should serve all political parties alike. This does not mean, however, that he should not exercise his franchise and vote as he wishes at local government elections, but he should not be a 'party' man, otherwise his advice might be regarded as being tainted and the council as a whole, in the end, would cease to have confidence in his advice.

As an executive his functions must be exercised impartially and he must carry out the policy decided by the council free from any political bias. In this respect English local government differs from Continental and American local government where officials are appointed, not because of their absence of political views but because of the strength of their political views. In these countries, it is therefore quite common for certain officials to change if political control of the council changes.

The principal officers of a local authority are those which the authority decides to appoint. In the case of a local council, the only official may be the clerk. Before the 1972 Act, it was usual for principal authorities to have a fairly standard pattern of senior officials – a medical officer of health, an engineer and surveyor, a chief education officer and so on, but there has been a development towards different breakdowns of functions and new titles. There has been a perhaps unfortunate tendency for grander and longer titles for officials.

Chief executive of the council

He is the chief executive and administrative officer of the local authority, and it is to him in the end that the council must turn to see that its decisions are executed. He often acts as secretary of the local authority and is generally responsible for convening all the meetings of the local authority and its committees. He is responsible for presenting to the council and its committees all matters of business which are brought to his notice, either from members of the public, members of the council or from the officers themselves, and of recording the decisions, either by way of minutes of the committees or reports of the committees which are subsequently presented to the council. The person appointed as chief executive should be chosen for his administrative ability, and a legal qualification, although extremely useful, is not essential.

The chief executive of the authority will from time to time report to the council and its committees on all legislation which is new and which affects the local authority. It is his overall responsibility to communicate with government departments on behalf of the authority, although in practice the appropriate chief officer will attend to this. The chief executive is responsible for the safe custody of all the council's books of record, documents of title and the common seal. He must have a full knowledge of the local bye-laws, local Acts of Parliament and Standing Orders of the council, so that he may be in a position at any time to advise the local authority on its functions and powers. He, or a deputy on his behalf, will invariably attend or will be represented at all meetings of the council, its committees and sub-committees.

As co-ordinator of the council's work he will be brought daily into contact with the council's officers to whom he should become guide, counsellor and friend. When the council's officers work together as a team, there is a greater chance that the authority will run smoothly.

Treasurer or chief financial officer

Even a local council has to have an officer responsible for the administration of its financial affairs although this duty may well fall upon the clerk. His duties are to prepare the estimates of expenditure for all committees of the council after the council has formulated its policy. He must prepare for payment all accounts due from the local authority and must collect for the authority all sums due from time to time to the local authority particularly in regard to the collection of Council Tax and rates.

His duties are not merely mechanical. Finance plays a very great part in modern local government and a skilful treasurer with an appreciation of modern accountancy practices and legislation can effect great financial savings to the local authority which he serves. The treasurer's work has now become so specialised that persons of the highest professional expertise are required to fill this office and the extent of personal responsibility is considerable. He must control the spending of money by the local authority and draw the attention of the authority to proposed expenditure which is in excess of its estimates.

Monitoring officer

A principal council is required by section 5 of the LGHA 1989 (as amended by the LGA 2000) to designate one of its officers as the monitoring officer (he cannot be the chief executive officer). His duty is to investigate and report to the council on any possible breaches of the law or of any code of practice by the council or its committees or officers. He maintains the register of interests of both his own councillors and those of the members of local councils within the area of his council. He is also required to monitor possible instances of maladministration which might give rise to a complaint to the local ombudsman (see Chapter 10).

The monitoring officer will be closely involved in the investigations by the Standards Board and Welsh local ombudsman into allegations of failure to comply with the council's code of conduct (see Chapter 11).

Other officers

The number and designation of other principal officers of a local authority will naturally vary with the functions which each class of local authority is called upon to carry out, although some officers must be appointed by statute, e.g. Directors of Social Services, where the local authority has the relevant function.

The councillor should become acquainted with the principal officers of his authority from whom he can gain a considerable amount of information and help.

The relationship between councillors and officers

Councillors should be in no doubt that they and the officers of the local authority *must* work as a team for the benefit of the community they both serve. Their efforts are joint efforts. Whilst the councillors determine policy, they cannot do this to the full without the constant advice and help of the officers. Local government is their profession and their life and they are most helpful to the elected members. Use them, consult them, seek their advice and it will surprise the newly-elected councillor how much help and "know-how" he will receive.

It may be useful also to refer to the Model Code of Conduct, paragraph 6 (Appendix A, *post*).

Most larger authorities now provide secretarial and other support services for members to enable them to fulfill their aspirations. Elected member training is now commonplace not only in the period immediately following an election but in the best run councils it is ongoing. Members are no longer left to fend for themselves and those without the backing of a political group can rest assured that their officers are there to help not hinder.

Employees' code of conduct

The Secretary of State has power under the LGA 2000 to issue a code of conduct for local government employees. The code will be deemed to be part of the employment contract of every "qualifying employee" (most employees of a local authority are "qualifying employees", with the exception of teachers and fire fighters).

The National Assembly for Wales has exercised its power to make the Code of Conduct (Qualifying Local Government Employees) (Wales) Order 2001 (S.I. 2001 No. 2280). The Secretary of State has not yet exercised his power in relation to England.

CHAPTER 15

LOCAL AUTHORITY ASSOCIATIONS

It is natural that the differing classes of local authorities have joined together to watch over their respective interests.

There are three main local government associations in England:

1. The Local Government Association (LGA) – this represents principal authorities.

2. The Association of London Government (ALG) – this represents London authorities.

3. The National Association of Local Councils (NALC) – this represents local councils.

The LGA and NALC also operate in Wales. However, the Welsh Local Government Association (WLGA) represents principal authorities in Wales in association with the LGA, and some local councils in Wales are members of the Wales Association of Community and Town Councils (WACTC), an independent body not associated with NALC.

In addition to the foregoing, the Association of Larger Local Councils draws its membership from larger local councils (where the population of the area of the council exceeds 10,000) in both England and Wales.

Membership of an association is voluntary but the great majority of councils join their appropriate association. Section 143 of the LGA 1972 gives authorities a specific power to pay subscriptions to local authority associations.

All the associations have a secretariat and function on similar lines to local authorities themselves. They have committees which are elected, directly or indirectly, by the members and which report back.

They are important bodies which are recognised by central government as the representatives of their authorities. They have a considerable influence on Parliament. They are often instrumental is introducing legislation into Parliament and in modifying the government's legislative proposals for local government. The LGA and the WLGA are also closely involved in the setting of the revenue support grant and other grants to local government (see Chapter 2).

The associations also bring their influence to bear on the National Assembly for Wales, to which most of the powers formerly exercised over local government by the Secretary of State for Wales have been devolved.

The LGA and the WLGA both hold an annual conference. It is usual for the chief executive of an authority to accompany councillor representatives to the annual conference. NALC holds an annual general meeting, a biennial national conference and an annual Welsh conference. WACTC holds an annual conference, as does the ALLC.

All the associations give legal and other advice to their member authorities and publish a wide range of information of relevance to them.

Although not a local authority association, the

Association of Councillors provides advice and assistance to councillors of all types of local authority.

The addresses of all the associations can be found in Appendix E.

STANDARDS OF CONDUCT

This Appendix contains—

(1) The Relevant Authorities (General Principles) Order 2001

(2) The Local Authorities (Model Code of Conduct) (England) Order 2001

(3) The Parish Councils (Model Code of Conduct) Order 2001

(4) The Relevant Authorities (Standards Committee) Regulations 2001

(1) THE RELEVANT AUTHORITIES (GENERAL PRINCIPLES) ORDER 2001
S.I. 2001 No. 1401

Made	*5th April 2001*
Coming into force	*6th April 2001*

The Secretary of State for the Environment, Transport and the Regions, in exercise of the powers conferred upon him by sections 49(1) and 105 of the Local Government Act 2000, and of all other powers enabling him in that behalf, and having carried out such consultation as is required by virtue of section 49(3) and (4) of that Act hereby makes the following Order, a draft of which has been laid before, and approved by a resolution of, each House of Parliament.

Citation and commencement

1. This Order may be cited as the Relevant Authorities (General Principles) Order 2001 and shall come into force on the day after the day on which it is made.

Interpretation

2.   In this Order—

"the Act" means the Local Government Act 2000;

"members" means members and co-opted members of relevant authorities; and

"statutory officers" means heads of paid service, chief finance officers and monitoring officers.

General principles

3.—(1)   The Secretary of State hereby specifies in the Schedule to this Order, the principles which are to govern the conduct of members of relevant authorities in England and police authorities in Wales.

(2)   Only paragraphs 2 and 8 of the Schedule to this Order shall have effect in relation to the activities of a member that are undertaken other than in an official capacity.

SCHEDULE
The General Principles

Selflessness

1.   Members should serve only the public interest and should never improperly confer an advantage or disadvantage on any person.

Honesty and Integrity

2.   Members should not place themselves in situations where their honesty and integrity may be questioned, should not behave improperly and should on all occasions avoid the appearance of such behaviour.

Objectivity

3.   Members should make decisions on merit, including when making appointments, awarding contracts or recommending individuals for rewards or benefits.

Accountability

4.   Members should be accountable to the public for their actions and the manner in which they carry out their responsibilities, and should co-operate fully and honestly with any scrutiny appropriate to their particular office.

Openness

5.   Members should be as open as possible about their actions and those of their authority, and should be prepared to give reasons for those actions.

Personal Judgement

6.   Members may take account of the views of others, including their political groups, but should reach their own conclusions on the issues before them and act in accordance with those conclusions.

Respect for Others

7.   Members should promote equality by not discriminating unlawfully against any person, and by treating people with respect, regardless of their race, age, religion, gender, sexual orientation or disability. They should respect the impartiality and integrity of the authority's statutory officers, and its other employees.

Duty to Uphold the Law

8.   Members should uphold the law and, on all occasions, act in accordance with the trust that the public is entitled to place in them.

Stewardship

9.   Members should do whatever they are able to do to ensure that their authorities use their resources prudently and in accordance with the law.

Leadership

10. Members should promote and support these principles

by leadership, and by example, and should act in a way that secures or preserves public confidence.

Note: Separate, but effectively identical, provision is made for councillors of local authorities in Wales by the Conduct of Members (Principles) (Wales) Order 2001 (S.I. 2001 No. 2276 (W.166)).

(2) THE LOCAL AUTHORITIES (MODEL CODE OF CONDUCT) (ENGLAND) ORDER 2001

S.I. 2001 No. 3575

Made	5th November 2001
Laid before Parliament	6th November 2001
Coming into force	27th November 2001

The Secretary of State for Transport, Local Government and the Regions, in exercise of the powers conferred upon him by sections 50(1) and (4), 81(2) and (3), and 105(2), (3) and (4) of the Local Government Act 2000, and of all other powers enabling him in that behalf, having carried out such consultation as is required by virtue of section 49 of that Act, and being satisfied that this order is consistent with the principles for the time being specified in an order under section 49(1) of that Act, hereby makes the following Order:

Citation, commencement and application

1.—(1) This Order may be cited as the Local Authorities (Model Code of Conduct) (England) Order 2001 and shall come into force on 27th November 2001.

(2) This Order applies in relation to these authorities in England—

(a) a county council;

(b) a district council;

(c) a London borough council;

(d) the Greater London Authority;

(e) the London Fire and Emergency Planning Authority;

(f) the Common Council of the City of London in its capacity as a local authority or police authority;

(g) the Council of the Isles of Scilly;

(h) a fire authority constituted by a combination scheme under the Fire Services Act 1947; and

(i) a joint authority established by Part IV of the Local Government Act 1985,

and references to "authority" shall be construed accordingly.

Model code of conduct — authorities operating executive arrangements

2.—(1) The Secretary of State hereby issues a model code as regards the conduct which is expected of members and co-opted members of authorities which are operating executive arrangements and that code is set out in Schedule 1 to this Order.

(2) For such authorities, all the provisions of the model code in Schedule 1 to this Order are mandatory.

(3) Where an authority which is not operating executive arrangements begins to do so, Schedule 1 to this Order shall have effect in relation to that authority as if it consisted of mandatory provisions of a model code of conduct issued in a subsequent order made under section 51(2) of the Local Government Act 2000 on the day on which the authority begins to operate those arrangements.

Model code of conduct — authorities not operating executive arrangements

3.—(1) The Secretary of State hereby issues a model code as regards the conduct which is expected of members and co-opted members of authorities which are not operating executive arrangements and that code is set out in Schedule 2 to this Order.

(2) For such authorities, all the provisions of the model code in Schedule 2 to this Order are mandatory.

(3) Where an authority which is operating executive

arrangements ceases to do so, Schedule 2 to this Order shall have effect in relation to that authority as if it consisted of mandatory provisions of a model code of conduct issued in a subsequent order made under section 51(2) of the Local Government Act 2000 on the day on which the authority ceases to operate those arrangements.

Transitional provision

4.–(1) On the day an authority's code of conduct is adopted or applied to it, the following shall, where applicable to the authority, be disapplied as respects that authority until 27th July 2002–

- (a) sections 94 to 98 and 105 of the Local Government Act 1972;

- (b) any order made under section 83 of the Local Government Act 1972;

- (c) section 30(3A) of the Local Government Act 1974;

- (d) any regulations made or code issued under sections 19 and 31 of the Local Government and Housing Act 1989;

- (e) in section 17 of the Audit Commission Act 1998, subsections (1)(b), (3), (5)(b), (7) and (8) and in subsection (2), the words "subject to subsection (3)" and paragraphs (a) and (b);

- (f) section 18 of the Audit Commission Act 1998;

- (g) any order made under section 28 of the Greater London Authority Act 1999; and

- (h) any guidance issued under section 66 of the Greater London authority Act 1999.

(2) Section 16(1) of the Interpretation Act 1978 shall apply to a disapplication under paragraph (1) above as if it were a repeal, by an Act, of an enactment.

SCHEDULE 1
The Model Code of Conduct — Authorities operating executive arrangements

PART 1
GENERAL PROVISIONS

Scope

1.—(1) A member must observe the authority's code of conduct whenever he—

(a) conducts the business of the authority;

(b) conducts the business of the office to which he has been elected or appointed; or

(c) acts as a representative of the authority,

and references to a member's official capacity shall be construed accordingly.

(2) An authority's code of conduct shall not, apart from paragraphs 4 and 5(a) below, have effect in relation to the activities of a member undertaken other than in an official capacity.

(3) Where a member acts as a representative of the authority—

(a) on another relevant authority, he must, when acting for that other authority, comply with that other authority's code of conduct; or

(b) on any other body, he must, when acting for that other body, comply with the authority's code of conduct, except and insofar as it conflicts with any other lawful obligations to which that other body may be subject.

(4) In this code, "member" includes a co-opted member of an authority.

General Obligations

2.   A member must—

(a) promote equality by not discriminating unlawfully against any person;

(b) treat others with respect; and

(c) not do anything which compromises or which is likely to compromise the impartiality of those who work for, or on behalf of, the authority.

3.   A member must not—

(a) disclose information given to him in confidence by anyone, or information acquired which he believes is of a confidential nature, without the consent of a person authorised to give it, or unless he is required by law to do so; nor

(b) prevent another person from gaining access to information to which that person is entitled by law.

4.   A member must not in his official capacity, or any other circumstance, conduct himself in a manner which could reasonably be regarded as bringing his office or authority into disrepute.

5.   A member—

(a) must not in his official capacity, or any other circumstance, use his position as a member improperly to confer on or secure for himself or any other person, an advantage or disadvantage; and

(b) must, when using or authorising the use by others of the resources of the authority—

(i) act in accordance with the authority's requirements; and

(ii) ensure that such resources are not used for political purposes unless that use could reasonably be regarded as likely to facilitate, or be conducive to, the discharge of the functions of the authority or of the office to which the member has been elected or appointed.

6.—(1) A member must when reaching decisions—

(a) have regard to any relevant advice provided to him by—

   (i) the authority's chief finance officer acting in pursuance of his duties under section 114 of the Local Government Finance Act 1988; and

   (ii) the authority's monitoring officer acting in pursuance of his duties under section 5(2) of the Local Government and Housing Act 1989; and

(b) give the reasons for those decisions in accordance with the authority's and any statutory requirements in relation to the taking of an executive decision.

(2) In sub-paragraph (1)(b) above and in paragraph 9(2) below, "executive decision" is to be construed in accordance with any regulations made by the Secretary of State under section 22 of the Local Government Act 2000.

7.   A member must, if he becomes aware of any conduct by another member which he reasonably believes involves a failure to comply with the authority's code of conduct, make a written allegation to that effect to the Standards Board for England as soon as it is practicable for him to do so.

PART 2
INTERESTS

Personal Interests

8.—(1)   A member must regard himself as having a personal interest in any matter if the matter relates to an interest in respect of which notification must be given under paragraphs 14 and 15 below, or if a decision upon it might reasonably be regarded as affecting to a greater extent than other council tax payers, ratepayers or inhabitants of the authority's area, the well-being or financial position of himself, a relative or a friend or—

(a) any employment or business carried on by such persons;

(b) any person who employs or has appointed such persons, any firm in which they are a partner, or any company of which they are directors;

(c) any corporate body in which such persons have a beneficial interest in a class of securities exceeding the nominal value of £5,000; or

(d) any body listed in sub-paragraphs (a) to (e) of paragraph 15 below in which such persons hold a position of general control or management.

(2) In this paragraph—

(a) "relative" means a spouse, partner, parent, parent-in-law, son, daughter, step-son, step-daughter, child of a partner, brother, sister, grandparent, grandchild, uncle, aunt, nephew, niece, or the spouse or partner of any of the preceding persons; and

(b) "partner" in sub-paragraph (2)(a) above means a member of a couple who live together.

Disclosure of Personal Interests

9.—(1) A member with a personal interest in a matter who attends a meeting of the authority at which the matter is considered must disclose to that meeting the existence and nature of that interest at the commencement of that consideration, or when the interest becomes apparent.

(2) Subject to paragraph 12(1)(b) below, a member with

a personal interest in any matter who has made an executive decision in relation to that matter must ensure that any written statement of that decision records the existence and nature of that interest.

Prejudicial Interests

10.—(1) Subject to sub-paragraph (2) below, a member with a personal interest in a matter also has a prejudicial interest in that matter if the interest is one which a member of the public with knowledge of the relevant facts would reasonably regard as so significant that it is likely to prejudice the member's judgement of the public interest.

(2) A member may regard himself as not having a prejudicial interest in a matter if that matter relates to—

(a) another relevant authority of which he is a member;

(b) another public authority in which he holds a position of general control or management;

(c) a body to which he has been appointed or nominated by the authority as its representative;

(d) the housing functions of the authority where the member holds a tenancy or lease with a relevant authority, provided that he does not have arrears of rent with that relevant authority of more than two months, and provided that those functions do not relate particularly to the member's tenancy or lease;

(e) the functions of the authority in respect of school meals, transport and travelling expenses, where the member is a guardian or parent of a child in full time education, unless it relates particularly to the school which the child attends;

(f) the functions of the authority in respect of statutory sick pay under Part XI of the Social Security Contributions and Benefits Act 1992, where the member is in receipt of, or is entitled to the receipt of such pay from a relevant authority; and

(g) the functions of the authority in respect of an allowance or payment made under sections 173 to 176 of the Local Government Act 1972 or section 18 of the Local Government and Housing Act 1989.

Overview and Scrutiny Committees

11.—(1) For the purposes of this Part, a member must if he is involved in the consideration of a matter at a meeting of an overview and scrutiny committee of the authority or a sub-committee of such a committee, regard himself as having a personal and a prejudicial interest if that consideration relates to a decision made, or action taken, by another of the authority's—

(a) committees or sub-committees; or

(b) joint committees or joint sub-committees,

of which he may also be a member.

(2) But sub-paragraph (1) above shall not apply if that member attends that meeting for the purpose of answering questions or otherwise giving evidence relating to that decision or action.

Participation in Relation to Disclosed Interests

12.—(1) Subject to sub-paragraph (2) below, a member with a prejudicial interest in any matter must—

(a) withdraw from the room or chamber where a meeting is being held whenever it becomes apparent that the matter is being considered at that meeting, unless he has obtained a dispensation from the authority's standard's committee;

(b) not exercise executive functions in relation to that matter; and (c) not seek improperly to influence a decision about that matter.

(2) A member with a prejudicial interest may, unless that interest is of a financial nature, and unless it is an interest of the type described in paragraph 11 above, participate in a meeting of the authority's—

(a) overview and scrutiny committees; and

(b) joint or area committees,

to the extent that such committees are not exercising functions of the authority or its executive.

13. For the purposes of this Part, "meeting" means any meeting of—

(a) the authority;

(b) the executive of the authority; or

(c) any of the authority's or its executive's committees, sub-committees, joint committees, joint sub-committees, or area committees.

PART 3
THE REGISTER OF MEMBERS' INTERESTS

Registration of Financial and Other Interests

14. Within 28 days of the provisions of an authority's code of conduct being adopted or applied to that authority or within 28 days of his election or appointment to office (if that is later), a member must register his financial interests in the authority's register maintained under section 81(1) of the Local Government Act 2000 by providing written notification to the authority's monitoring officer of—

(a) any employment or business carried on by him;

(b) the name of the person who employs or has appointed him, the name of any firm in which he is a partner, and the name of any company for which he is a remunerated director;

(c) the name of any person, other than a relevant authority, who has made a payment to him in respect of his election or any expenses incurred by him in carrying out his duties;

(d) the name of any corporate body which has a place of business or land in the authority's area, and in which the member has a beneficial interest in a class of securities of that body that exceeds the nominal value of £25,000 or one hundredth of the total issued share capital of that body;

(e) a description of any contract for goods, services or works made between the authority and himself or a firm in which he is a partner, a company of which he is a remunerated director, or a body of the description specified in sub-paragraph (d) above;

(f) the address or other description (sufficient to identify the location) of any land in which he has a beneficial interest and which is in the area of the authority;

(g) the address or other description (sufficient to identify the location) of any land where the landlord is the authority and the tenant is a firm in which he is a partner, a company of which he is a remunerated director, or a body of the description specified in sub-paragraph (d) above; and

(h) the address or other description (sufficient to identify the location) of any land in the authority's area in which he has a licence (alone or jointly with others) to occupy for 28 days or longer.

15. Within 28 days of the provisions of the authority's code of conduct being adopted or applied to that authority or within 28 days of his election or appointment to office (if that is later), a member must register his other interests in the authority's register maintained under section 81(1) of the

Local Government Act 2000 by providing written notification to the authority's monitoring officer of his membership of or position of general control or management in any—

(a) body to which he has been appointed or nominated by the authority as its representative;

(b) public authority or body exercising functions of a public nature;

(c) company, industrial and provident society, charity, or body directed to charitable purposes;

(d) body whose principal purposes include the influence of public opinion or policy; and

(e) trade union or professional association.

16. A member must within 28 days of becoming aware of any change to the interests specified under paragraphs 14 and 15 above, provide written notification to the authority's monitoring officer of that change.

Registration of Gifts and Hospitality

17. A member must within 28 days of receiving any gift or hospitality over the value of £25, provide written notification to the authority's monitoring officer of the existence and nature of that gift or hospitality.

SCHEDULE 2
The Model Code of Conduct — Authorities not operating executive arrangements

PART 1
GENERAL PROVISIONS

Scope

1.—(1) A member must observe the authority's code of conduct whenever he—

(a) conducts the business of the authority;

(b) conducts the business of the office to which he has been elected or appointed; or

(c) acts as a representative of the authority,

and references to a member's official capacity shall be construed accordingly.

(2) An authority's code of conduct shall not, apart from paragraphs 4 and 5(a) below, have effect in relation to the activities of a member undertaken other than in an official capacity.

(3) Where a member acts as a representative of the authority—

(a) on another relevant authority, he must, when acting for that other authority, comply with that other authority's code of conduct; or

(b) on any other body, he must, when acting for that other body, comply with the authority's code of conduct, except and insofar as it conflicts with any other lawful obligations to which that other body may be subject.

(4) In this code, "member" includes a co-opted member of an authority.

General Obligations

2. A member must—

(a) promote equality by not discriminating unlawfully against any person;

(b) treat others with respect; and

(c) not do anything which compromises or which is likely to compromise the impartiality of those who work for, or on behalf of, the authority.

3. A member must not—

(a) disclose information given to him in confidence by anyone, or information acquired which he believes is of a confidential nature, without the consent of a person authorised to give it, or unless he is required by law to do so; nor

(b) prevent another person from gaining access to information to which that person is entitled by law.

4. A member must not in his official capacity, or any other circumstance, conduct himself in a manner which could reasonably be regarded as bringing his office or authority into disrepute.

5. A member—

(a) must not be in his official capacity, or any other circumstance, use his position as a member improperly to confer on or secure for himself or any other person, an advantage or disadvantage; and

(b) must, when using or authorising the use by others of the resources of the authority,—

(i) act in accordance with the authority's requirements; and

(ii) ensure that such resources are not used for political purposes

unless that use could reasonably be regarded as likely to facilitate, or be conducive to, the discharge of the functions of the authority or of the office to which the member has been elected or appointed.

6. A member must when reaching decisions have regard to any relevant advice provided to him by—

(a) the authority's chief finance officer acting in pursuance of his duties under section 114 of the Local Government Finance Act 1988 or an equivalent provision in any regulations made under section 6(6) of the Local Government and Housing Act 1989; and

(b) the authority's monitoring officer acting in pursuance of his duties under section 5(2) of the Local Government and Housing Act 1989.

7. A member must, if he becomes aware of any conduct by another member which he reasonably believes involves a failure to comply with the authority's code if conduct, make a written allegation to that effect to the Standards Board for England as soon as it is practicable for him to do so.

PART 2
INTERESTS

Personal Interests

8.—(1) A member must regard himself as having a personal interest in any matter if the matter relates to an interest in respect of which notification must be given under paragraphs 13 and 14 below, or if a decision upon it might reasonably be regarded as affecting to a greater extent than other council tax payers, ratepayers, or inhabitants of the authority's area, the well-being or financial position of himself, a relative or a friend or—

(a) any employment or business carried on by such persons;

(b) any person who employs or has appointed such persons, any firm in which they are a partner, or any company of which they are directors;

(c) any corporate body in which such persons have a beneficial interest in a class of securities exceeding the nominal value of £5,000; or

(d) any body listed in sub-paragraphs (a) to (e) of paragraph 14 below in which such persons hold a position of general control or management.

(2) In this paragraph—

(a) "relative" means a spouse, partner, parent, parent-in-law, son, daughter, step-son, step-daughter, child of a partner, brother, sister, grandparent, grandchild, uncle, aunt, nephew, niece, or the spouse or partner of any of the preceding persons; and

(b) "partner" in sub-paragraph (2)(a) above means a member of a couple who live together.

Disclosure of Personal Interests

9.   A member with a personal interest in a matter who attends a meeting of the authority at which the matter is considered must disclose to that meeting the existence and nature of that interest at the commencement of that consideration, or when the interest becomes apparent.

Prejudicial Interests

1.—(1) Subject to sub-paragraph (2) below, a member with a personal interest in a matter also has a prejudicial interest in that matter if the interest is one which a member of the public with knowledge of the relevant facts would reasonably regard as so significant that it is likely to prejudice the member's judgement of the public interest.

(2) A member may regard himself as not having a prejudicial interest in a matter if that matter relates to—

(a) another relevant authority of which he is a member;

(b) another public authority in which he holds a position of general control or management;

(c) a body to which he has been appointed or nominated by the authority as its representative;

(d) the housing functions of the authority where the member holds a tenancy or lease with a relevant authority, provided that he does not have arrears of rent with that relevant authority of more than two months, and provided that those functions do not relate particularly to the member's tenancy or lease;

(e) the functions of the authority in respect of school meals, transport and travelling expenses, where the member is a guardian or parent of a child in full time education, unless it relates particularly to the school which the child attends;

(f) the functions of the authority in respect of statutory sick pay under Part XI of the Social Security Contributions and Benefits Act 1992, where the member is in receipt of, or is entitled to the receipt of such pay from a relevant authority; and

(g) any functions of the authority in respect of an allowance or payment made under sections 173 to 176 of the Local Government Act 1972 or section 18 of the Local Government and Housing Act 1989.

Participation in Relation to Disclosed Interests

11. A member with a prejudicial interest in any matter must—

(a) withdraw from the room or chamber where a meeting is being held whenever it becomes apparent that the matter is being considered at that meeting, unless he has obtained a dispensation from the authority's standards committee; and

(b) not seek improperly to influence a decision about that matter.

12. For the purposes of this Part, "meeting" means any meeting of—

(a) the authority; or

(b) any of the authority's committees, sub-committees,

joint committees, joint sub-committees, or advisory committees.

PART 3
THE REGISTER OF MEMBERS' INTERESTS

Registration of Financial and Other Interests

13. Within 28 days of the provisions of an authority's code of conduct being adopted or applied to that authority or within 28 days of his election or appointment to office (if that is later), a member must register his financial interests in the authority's register maintained under section 81(1) of the Local Government Act 2000 by providing written notification to the authority's monitoring officer of—

(a) any employment or business carried on by him;

(b) the name of the person who employs or has appointed him, the name of any firm in which he is a partner, and the name of any company for which he is a remunerated director;

(c) the name of any person, other than a relevant authority, who has made a payment to him in respect of his election or any expenses incurred by him in carrying out his duties;

(d) the name of any corporate body which has a place of business or land in the authority's area, and in which the member has a beneficial interest in a class of securities of that body that exceeds the nominal value of £25,000 or one hundredth of the total issued share capital of that body;

(e) a description of any contract for goods, services or works made between the authority and himself or a firm in which he is a partner, a company of which he is a remunerated director, or a body of the description specified in sub-paragraph (d) above;

(f) the address or other description (sufficient to identify the location) of any land in which he has a beneficial interest and which is in the area of the authority;

(g) the address or other description (sufficient to identify the location) of any land where the landlord is the authority and the tenant is a firm in which he is a partner, a company of which he is a remunerated director, or a body of the description specified in sub-paragraph (d) above; and

(h) the address or other description (sufficient to identify the location) of any land in the authority's area in which he has a licence (alone or jointly with others) to occupy for 28 days or longer.

14. Within 28 days of the provisions of the authority's code of conduct being adopted or applied to that authority or within 28 days of his election or appointment to office (if that is later), a member must register his other interests in the authority's register maintained under section 81(1) of the Local Government Act 2000 by providing written notification to the authority's monitoring officer of his membership of or position of general control or management in any—

(a) body to which he has been appointed or nominated by the authority as its representative;

(b) public authority or body exercising functions of a public nature;

(c) company, industrial and provident society, charity, or body directed to charitable purposes;

(d) body whose principal purposes include the influence of public opinion or policy; and

(e) trade union or professional association.

15. A member must within 28 days of becoming aware of any changes to the interests specified under paragraphs 13

and 14 above, provide written notification to the authority's monitoring officer of that change.

Registration of Gifts and Hospitality

16. A member must within 28 days of receiving any gift or hospitality over the value of £25, provide written notification to the authority's monitoring officer of the existence and nature of that gift or hospitality.

Note: Separate, but effectively identical, provision is made for councillors of local authorities in Wales by the Conduct of Members (Model Code of Conduct) (Wales) Order 2001 (S.I. 2001 No. 2289 (W.177)).

(3) THE PARISH COUNCILS (MODEL CODE OF CONDUCT) ORDER 2001
S.I. 2001 No. 3576

Made	*5th November 2001*
Laid before Parliament	*6th November 2001*
Coming into force	*27th November 2001*

The Secretary of State for Transport, Local Government and the Regions, in exercise of the powers conferred upon him by sections 50(1) and (4), 81(2) and (3), and 105(2), (3) and (4) of the Local Government Act 2000, and of all other powers enabling him in that behalf, having carried out such consultation as is required by virtue of section 49 of that Act, and being satisfied that this Order is consistent with the principles for the time being specified in an order under section 49(1) of that Act, hereby makes the following Order:

Citation, commencement and application

1.—(1) This Order may be cited as the Parish Councils (Model Code of Conduct) Order 2001 and shall come into force on 27th November 2001.

(2) This Order applies in relation to parish councils, and references to "authority" shall be construed accordingly.

Model code of conduct – parish councils

2.—(1) The Secretary of State hereby issues a model code as regards the conduct which is expected of members and co-opted members of authorities and that code is set out in the Schedule to this Order.

(2) All the provisions of the model code in the Schedule to this Order are mandatory.

Transitional provision

3.–(1) On the day an authority's code of conduct is adopted or applied to it, the following shall, where applicable to the authority, be disapplied as respects that authority until 27th July 2002—

(a) sections 94 to 98 and 105 of the Local Government Act 1972;

(b) any order made under section 83 of the Local Government Act 1972;

(c) any regulations made or code issued under sections 19 and 31 of the Local Government and Housing Act 1989;

(d) in section 17 of the Audit Commission Act 1998, subsections (1)(b), (3), (5)(b), (7) and (8) and in subsection (2), the words "subject to subsection (3)" and paragraphs (a) and (b);

(e) section 18 of the Audit Commission Act 1998;

(2) Section 16(1) of the Interpretation Act 1978 shall apply to a disapplication under paragraph (1) above as if it were a repeal, by an Act, of an enactment.

SCHEDULE
The Model Code of Conduct — Parish councils

PART 1
GENERAL PROVISIONS

Scope

1.–(1) A member must observe the authority's code of conduct whenever he—

(a) conducts the business of the authority;

(b) conducts the business of the office to which he has been elected or appointed; or

(c) acts as a representative of the authority,

and references to a member's official capacity shall be construed accordingly.

(2) An authority's code of conduct shall not, apart from paragraphs 4 and 5(a) below, have effect in relation to the activities of a member undertaken other than in an official capacity.

(3) Where a member acts as a representative of the authority—

(a) on another relevant authority, he must, when acting for that other authority, comply with that other authority's code of conduct; or

(b) on any other body, he must, when acting for that other body, comply with the authority's code of conduct, except and insofar as it conflicts with any other lawful obligations to which that other body may be subject.

(4) In this code—

(a) "member" includes a co-opted member of an authority; and

(b) "responsible authority" means a district council or a unitary county council which has functions in relation to the parish councils for which it is responsible under section 55(12) of the Local Government Act 2000.

General Obligations

2. A member must—

(a) promote equality by not discriminating unlawfully against any person;

(b) treat others with respect; and

(c) not do anything which compromises or which is likely

to compromise the impartiality of those who work for, or on behalf of, the authority.

3.   A member must not—

(a) disclose information given to him in confidence by anyone, or information acquired which he believes is of a confidential nature, without the consent of a person authorised to give it, or unless he is required by law to do so; nor

(b) prevent another person from gaining access to information to which that person is entitled by law.

4.   A member must not in his official capacity, or any other circumstance, conduct himself in a manner which could reasonably be regarded as bringing his office or authority into disrepute.

5.   A member—

(a) must not in his official capacity, or any other circumstance, use his position as a member improperly to confer on or secure for himself or any other person, an advantage or disadvantage; and

(b) must, when using or authorising the use by others of the resources of the authority—

   (i) act in accordance with the authority's requirements; and

   (ii) ensure that such resources are not used for political purposes

unless that use could reasonably be regarded as likely to facilitate, or be conductive to, the discharge of the functions of the authority or of the office to which the member has been elected or appointed.

6.   A member must, if he becomes aware of any conduct by another member which he reasonably believes involves a

failure to comply with the authority's code of conduct, make a written allegation to that effect to the Standards Board for England as soon as it is practicable for him to do so.

PART 2
INTERESTS

Personal Interests

7.—(1)   A member must regard himself as having a personal interest in any matter if the matter relates to an interest in respect of which notification must be given under paragraphs 12 and 13 below, or if a decision upon it might reasonably be regarded as affecting to a greater extent than other council tax payers, ratepayers, or inhabitants of the authority's area, the well-being or financial position of himself, a relative or a friend or—

(a) any employment or business carried on by such persons;

(b) any person who employs or has appointed such persons, any firm in which they are a partner, or any company of which they are directors;

(c) any corporate body in which such persons have a beneficial interest in a class of securities exceeding the nominal value of £5,000; or

(d) any body listed in sub-paragraphs (a) to (e) of paragraph 13 below in which such persons hold a position of general control or management.

(2) In this paragraph—

(a) "relative" means a spouse, partner, parent, parent-in-law, son, daughter, step-son, step-daughter, child of a partner, brother, sister, grandparent, grandchild, uncle, aunt, nephew, niece, or the spouse or partner of any of the preceding persons; and

(b) "partner" in sub-paragraph (2)(a) above means a member of a couple who live together.

Disclosure of Personal Interests

8. A member with a personal interest in a matter who attends a meeting of the authority at which the matter is considered must disclose to that meeting the existence and nature of that interest at the commencement of that consideration, or when the interest becomes apparent.

Prejudicial Interests

9.—(1) Subject to sub-paragraph (2) below, a member with a personal interest in a matter also has a prejudicial interest in that matter if the interest is one which a member of the public with knowledge of the relevant facts would reasonably regard as so significant that it is likely to prejudice the member's judgement of the public interest.

(2) A member may regard himself as not having a prejudicial interest in a matter if that matter relates to—

(a) another relevant authority of which he is a member;

(b) another public authority in which he holds a position of general control or management;

(c) a body to which he has been appointed or nominated by the authority as its representative;

(d) any functions of the authority in respect of statutory sick pay under Part XI of the Social Security Contributions and Benefits Act 1992, where the member is in receipt of, or is entitled to the receipt of such pay from a relevant authority; and

(e) any functions of the authority in respect of an allowance or payment made under sections 173 to 173A and 175 to 176 of the Local Government Act

1972 or section 18 of the Local Government and Housing Act 1989.

Participation in Relation to Disclosed Interests

10. A member with a prejudicial interest in any matter must—

(a) withdraw from the room or chamber where a meeting is being held whenever it becomes apparent that the matter is being considered at that meeting, unless he has obtained a dispensation from the standards committee of the responsible authority; and

(b) not seek improperly to influence a decision about that matter.

11. For the purposes of this Part, "meeting" means any meeting of—

(a) the authority; or

(b) any of the authority's committees, sub-committees, joint committees or joint sub-committees.

PART 3
THE REGISTER OF MEMBERS' INTERESTS

Registration of Financial and Other Interests

12. Within 28 days of the provisions of an authority's code of conduct being adopted or applied to that authority or within 28 days of his election or appointment to office (if that is later), a member must register his financial interests in the authority's register maintained under section 81(1) of the Local Government Act 2000 by providing written notification to the monitoring officer of the responsible authority of—

(a) any employment or business carried on by him;

(b) the name of the person who employs or has appointed him, the name of any firm in which he is a partner, and the name of any company for which he is a remunerated director;

(c) the name of any person, other than a relevant authority, who has made a payment to him in respect of his election or any expenses incurred by him in carrying out his duties;

(d) the name of any corporate body which has a place of business or land in the authority's area, and in which the member has a beneficial interest in a class of securities of that body that exceeds the nominal value of £25,000 or one hundredth of the total issued share capital of that body;

(e) a description of any contract for goods, services or works made between the authority and himself or a firm in which he is a partner, a company of which he is a remunerated director, or a body of the description specified in sub-paragraph (d) above;

(f) the address or other description (sufficient to identify the location) of any land in which he has a beneficial interest and which is in the area of the authority;

(g) the address or other description (sufficient to identify the location) of any land where the landlord is the authority and the tenant is a firm in which he is a partner, a company of which he is a remunerated director, or a body of the description specified in sub-paragraph (d) above; and

(h) the address or other description (sufficient to identify the location) of any land in the authority's area in which he has a licence (alone or jointly with others) to occupy for 28 days or longer.

13. Within 28 days of the provisions of the authority's code of conduct being adopted or applied to that authority or within 28 days of his election or appointment to office (if that

is later), a member must register his other interests in the authority's register maintained under section 81(1) of the Local Government Act 2000 by providing written notification to the monitoring officer of the responsible authority of his membership of or position of general control or management in any—

    (a) body to which he has been appointed or nominated by the authority as its representative;

    (b) public authority or body exercising functions of a public nature;

    (c) company, industrial and provident society, charity, or body directed to charitable purposes;

    (d) body whose principal purposes include the influence of public opinion or policy; and

    (e) trade union or professional association.

14. A member must within 28 days of becoming aware of any change to the interests specified under paragraphs 12 and 13 above, provide written notification to the monitoring officer of the responsible authority of that change.

Registration of Gifts and Hospitality

15. A member must within 28 days of receiving any gift or hospitality over the value of £25, provide written notification to the monitoring officer of the responsible authority of the existence and nature of that gift or hospitality.

Note: There is no Welsh equivalent to the foregoing regulations. The code of conduct for community and town councillors in Wales is contained in the Conduct of Members (Model Code of Conduct) (Wales) Order 2001, noted *ante*, page 79.

(4) THE RELEVANT AUTHORITIES (STANDARDS COMMITTEE) REGULATIONS 2001
S.I. 2001 No. 2812[1]

Made	*1st August 2001*
Laid before Parliament	*7th August 2001*
Coming into force	*28th August 2001*

The Secretary of State for Transport, Local Government and the Regions, in exercise of the powers conferred upon him by sections 53(6) and (12), 55(8) and 105 of the Local Government Act 2000, and of all other powers enabling him in that behalf, hereby makes the following Regulations:

Citation, commencement and application

1.—(1) These Regulations may be cited as the Relevant Authorities (Standards Committee) Regulations 2001 and shall come into force on 28th August 2001.

(2) These Regulations apply in relation to relevant authorities in England, other than parish councils, and to police authorities in Wales, and references to "authority" shall be construed accordingly.

Interpretation

2. In these Regulations—

"the 1972 Act" means the Local Government Act 1972;

"the Act" means the Local Government Act 2000;

"independent member" means a person appointed to a standards committee, or sub-committee of the standards committee, of an authority under section 53(4)(b) or 55(7)(a) of the Act;

---

[1] The equivalent Welsh legislation is the Standards Committees (Wales) Regulations 2001 (S.I. 2001 No. 2283 (W.172)).

"partner" means a member of a couple who live together;

"relative" means a spouse, partner, parent, parent-in-law, son, daughter, step-son, step-daughter, brother, sister, grandparent, grandchild, uncle, aunt, nephew, niece, or the spouse or partner of any of the preceding persons; and

"responsible authority" means a district council or unitary county council which has functions in relation to the parish councils for which it is responsible under section 55(12) of the Act.

Size and composition of standards committees

3.—(1) An authority must ensure that—

(a) where its standards committee has more than three members, at least 25% are independent members; and

(b) where it is operating executive arrangements under Part II of the Act, no more than one member of its standards committee is a member of the executive.

(2) Where an authority is a responsible authority, it must ensure that—

(a) if its standards committee has appointed a sub-committee under section 55(3) of the Act, that standards committee includes at least one member of any of the parish councils for which the authority is the responsible authority; and

(b) a member of its standards committee, or sub-committee of the standards committee, appointed under sub-paragraph (a), or under section 55(6)(a) or 55(7)(b) of the Act, is not also a member of that responsible authority.

Appointment of independent member

4.   Subject to regulation 5(c), a person may not be appointed as an independent member of a standards committee of an authority or sub-committee of the standards committee unless the appointment is—

(a) approved by a majority of the members of the authority;

(b) advertised in one or more newspapers circulating in the area of the authority;

(c) of a person who has submitted an application to the authority;

(d) of a person who has not within the period of five years immediately preceding the date of the appointment been a member or officer of the authority; and

(e) of a person who is not a relative or close friend of a member or officer of the authority.

Transitional provision for independent members

5.   Where an authority has before the date on which these Regulations come into force established a committee, which has among its functions that of promoting and maintaining high standards of conduct by the members and co-opted members of the authority, and which includes any person who is not a member or officer of that or any other relevant authority—

(a) that committee may be treated by the authority as if it were a standards committee for the purposes of the Act;

(b) subject to sub-paragraph (c), these Regulations shall apply to that committee; and

(c) regulation 4 shall not apply to that committee until the end of the period of two years beginning with the date on which these Regulations come into force.

Validity of proceedings

6.—(1) Subject to paragraph (2), a meeting of a standards committee or sub-committee of a standards committee shall not be quorate unless at least three members (including at least one independent member) of that committee or sub-committee are present for its duration.

(2) Where at least one independent member would have been present for the duration of the meeting but for the fact that he was prevented or restricted from participating in any business of the authority by virtue of its code of conduct, the requirement in paragraph (2) for the quorum to include at least one independent member shall not apply.

Application of the Local Government Act 1972

7.—(1) Subject to paragraphs (2) and (3), Part VA of the 1972 Act shall apply in relation to meetings of a standards committee, or sub-committee of a standards committee, of an authority as it applies to meetings of a principal council.

(2) Sections 100E, 100G, 100J, and 100K of the 1972 Act shall not be so applied.

(3) Where a responsible authority must act in accordance with sections 100A(6)(a), 100B(1) or 100C(1) of the 1972 Act by virtue of paragraph (1), it shall also give to every parish council for which it is responsible—

(a) written notice of the time and place of the meeting at least three clear days before that meeting or, if the meeting is convened at shorter notice, then at the time it is convened;

(b) a copy of the agenda for a meeting and copies of any report for a meeting at least three clear days before the meeting, except that—

(i) where the meeting is convened at shorter notice, the copies of the agenda and reports shall be given to the parish council from the time the meeting is convened; and

(ii) where an item is added to an agenda, copies of which have been given to the parish council, copies of the item (or of the revised agenda), and the copies of any report for the meeting relating to the item shall be given to the parish council from the time the item is added to the agenda,

but nothing in this sub-paragraph requires copies of any agenda, item or report to be given to the parish council until copies are available to members of the responsible authority;

(c) after the meeting, a copy of the minutes excluding so much of the minutes of proceedings during which the meeting was not open to the public under section 100A(4) of the 1972 Act, or where applicable, a copy of a summary made under section 100C(2) of that Act;

(d) after the meeting, a copy of the agenda for the meeting; and

(e) after the meeting, a copy of so much of any report for the meeting as relates to any item during which the meeting was open to the public.

MEMBERS' ALLOWANCES

This Appendix contains—

(1) Section 18 of the Local Government and Housing Act 1989 (as amended by the Local Government Act 2000)

(2) Section 100 of the Local Government Act 2000

(3) Sections 173-178 of the Local Government Act 1972 (as amended)

(4) The Local Authorities (Members' Allowances) Regulations 1991 (as amended)

(5) The Local Authorities (Members' Allowances) (England) Regulations 2001

(6) Rates of travelling and subsistence allowances

(1) SECTION 18 OF THE LOCAL GOVERNMENT AND HOUSING ACT 1989 (as amended)

Schemes for basic, attendance and special responsibility allowances for local authority members

18.—(1) Subject to subsection (1A), the Secretary of State may by regulations authorise or require any such relevant authority as may be specified or described in the regulations to make a scheme providing for the payment of—

(a) a basic allowance for every member of the authority who is a councillor;

(b) an attendance allowance in relation to the carrying out by any such member of such duties as may be specified in or determined under the regulations; and

(c) a special responsibility allowance for any such member who has such special responsibilities in relation to the authority as may be so specified or determined.

(1A) In relation to a district council, county council, county borough council or London borough council, subsection (1) above shall have effect with the omission of paragraph (b).

(2) Regulations under this section may also authorise or require a scheme made by a relevant authority under the regulations to include provision for the payment to appointed members of allowances in respect of such losses of earnings and expenses as—

(a) are necessarily sustained or incurred in the carrying out, in connection with their membership of the authority or any committee or sub-committee of the authority, of duties specified in or determined under the regulations; and

(b) are not of a description in respect of which provision is made for an allowance under any of sections 174 to 176 of the Local Government Act 1972 or sections 46 to 48 of the Local Government (Scotland) Act 1973.

(2A) Regulations under this section may authorise or require a scheme made by a district council, a county council, county borough council or London borough council to include provision for the payment to members of the council allowances in respect of such expenses of arranging for the care of children or dependants as are necessarily incurred in the carrying out of their duties as members.

(3) Without prejudice to the generality of the powers conferred by subsections (1) to (2A) above, regulations under this section may contain such provision as the Secretary of State considers appropriate for requiring a scheme made by a relevant authority under the regulations—

(a) to make it a condition of any payment by way of allowance that, in the financial year to which the payment would relate, the aggregate amount which the authority has paid out or is already liable to pay out under the scheme does not exceed such maximum amount as may be specified in or determined under the regulations;

(b) to make provision for different maximum amounts to be applicable, for the purposes of any such condition, in relation to different allowances or in relation to different members or members of different groups;

(c) to make provision in relation to claims which cannot be paid by virtue of any such condition and provision for the payment to members of the authority who are councillors of an amount by way of supplement to the basic allowance where, in any financial year, the aggregate paid out or owing under the scheme is less than an amount specified in or determined under the regulations;

(d) to provide that the amount authorised by virtue of subsection (2) above to be paid by way of allowance in any case shall not exceed such amount as may be so specified or determined;

(e) to contain such provision as may be so specified or determined with respect to the general administration of the scheme, with respect to the manner in which, time within which and forms on which claims for any allowance are to be made and with respect to the information to be provided in support of any such claim;

(f) to contain such provision as may be so specified or determined for avoiding the duplication of payments or of allowances, for determining the bodies by which payments of allowances are to be made and for the apportionment of payments between different bodies.

(3A) Regulations under this section may make provision for or in connection with—

(a) enabling district councils, county councils, county borough councils or London borough councils to determine which members of the council are to be entitled to pensions, allowances or gratuities;

(b) treating the basic allowance or the special responsibility allowance as amounts in respect of which such pensions, allowances or gratuities are payable.

(3B) Regulations under this section may make provision for or in connection with requiring a district council, county council, county borough council or London borough council to establish and maintain a panel which is to have such functions as may be specified in the regulations in relation to allowances, or pensions, allowances or gratuities, payable to members of the council.

(3C) Regulations under this section may make provision for or in connection with enabling a panel established by a body specified in the regulations to exercise such functions as may be specified in the regulations in relation to allowances, or pensions, allowances or gratuities, payable to members of such district councils, county councils or London borough councils in England as may be specified in the regulations.

(3D) Regulations under this section may make provision for or in connection with the establishment by the National Assembly for Wales on a permanent or temporary basis of a panel which is to have such functions as may be specified in the regulations in relation to allowances, or pensions, allowances or gratuities, payable to members of county councils and county borough councils in Wales.

(3E)   Regulations under subsection (3B) above may include provision—

- *(a)* with respect to the number of persons who may or must be appointed to the panel of a council;

- *(b)* with respect to the persons who may or must be appointed to the panel of a council;

- *(c)* for or in connection with the appointment by councils of joint panels.

(3F)   Regulations under subsection (3C) may include provision—

- *(a)* with respect to the number of persons who may or must be appointed to a panel mentioned in that subsection;

- *(b)* with respect to the persons who may or must be appointed to such a panel.

(3G)   Regulations under subsection (3B), (3C) or (3D) may include provision—

- *(a)* for or in connection with enabling a panel mentioned in that subsection to make recommendations to a council on the level of allowances payable to members of the council;

- *(b)* for or in connection with enabling such a panel to make recommendations to a council as to which members of the council are to be entitled to pensions, allowances or gratuities;

- *(c)* which permits different recommendations to be made in relation to different councils or descriptions of council.

(4)   Regulations under this section may—

- *(a)* prohibit the payment, otherwise than in accordance with sections 174 to 176 of the Local Government

Act 1972 or sections 46 to 48 of the Local Government (Scotland) Act 1973 or in such other cases as may be specified in the regulations, of any allowance to a member of a relevant authority who is a councillor or to any appointed member of a relevant authority;

(b) impose requirements on a relevant authority with respect to the publication, in the minutes of that authority or otherwise, of the details of amounts paid in pursuance of a scheme made under the regulations;

(ba) make provision with respect to the amendement, revocation or replacement of a scheme made by a relevant authority under the regulations; and

(c) contain such incidental provision and such supplemental, consequential and transitional provision in connection with the other provisions of the regulations as the Secretary of State considers appropriate.

(5) In this section "relevant authority" means—

(a) a local authority of any of the descriptions specified in any of the paragraphs of section 21(1) below, other than paragraphs (d), (g) and (j), or in section 21(2) below;

(b) any body on which a body which is a relevant authority by virtue of paragraph (a) above is represented and which is designated as a relevant authority for the purposes of this section by regulations made by the Secretary of State; or

(c) any appeal committee so designated which is constituted in accordance with paragraph 2 or 3 of Schedule 33 to the Education Act 1996;

and references in this section to an appointed member, in relation to a relevant authority, are references to any person who is a member of the authority without being a councillor or who is a member of one or more of the authority's committees or sub-committees without being a member of the authority.

(5A) In making or operating any scheme authorised or required by regulations under thus section, a district council, county council, county borough council or London borough council shall have regard to any guidance for the time being issued by the Secretary of State.

(6) In this section any reference to a councillor includes a reference to a member of the authority concerned who, in accordance with regulations under this section, is to be treated as if he were a councillor.

(2) SECTION 100 OF THE LOCAL GOVERNMENT ACT 2000

100.—(I) The Secretary of State may by regulations make provision with respect to—

(a) allowances payable to members of a parish council,

(b) travelling and subsistence allowances payable to members of such relevant authorities as may be prescribed,

(c) allowances payable to members of such relevant authorities as may be prescribed for attending conferences or meetings,

(d) the reimbursement of expenses incurred by members of such relevant authorities as may be prescribed.

(2) For the purposes of this section a member of a committee or subcommittee of a relevant authority is to be treated as a member of the authority.

(3) The provision which may be made under subsection (1)(b) includes provision with respect to allowances in respect of travel by bicycle or by any other non-motorised form of transport.

(4) The provision which may be made under this section includes provision which amends or repeals any provisions of sections 173 to 178 of the Local Government Act 1972.

(5) Before making any regulations under this section, the Secretary of State must consult such representatives of local government and such other persons (if any) as he considers appropriate.

(6) In this section—

"prescribed" means prescribed by regulations made by the Secretary of State, "relevant authority" means—

(a) a body specified in section 21(l) of the Local Government and Housing Act 1989,

(b) a body on which a body falling within paragraph (a) is represented,

(c) a parish council.

(7) In its application to Wales this section has effect as if—

(a) for any reference to the Secretary of State there were substituted a reference to the National Assembly for Wales,

(b) for any reference to a parish council there were substituted a reference to a community council.

(3) SECTIONS 173 TO 178 OF THE LOCAL GOVERNMENT ACT 1972 (as amended)

Attendance allowance and financial loss allowance

173.—(1) Subject to subsection (6) below, any member of a parish or community who is a councillor shall be entitled to receive a payment by way of attendance allowance, that is to say, a payment for the performance of any approved duty, being a payment of such reasonable amount, not exceeding the prescribed amount, as the parish or community may determine unless a notice under section 173A below is effective in relation to him.

(2) The amount prescribed under subsection (1) above may be prescribed by reference to any period of twenty-four hours.

(3) The amount of any allowance determined by a parish or community under subsection (1) above may vary according to the time of day and the duration of the duty, but shall be the same for all members of the council entitled to the allowance in respect of a duty of any description at the same time of day and of the same duration.

(4) Subject to subsection (6) below, any member of a parish or community who is not entitled under subsection (1) above to receive attendance allowance for the performance of an approved duty shall be entitled to receive a payment by way of financial loss allowance, that is to say, a payment not exceeding the prescribed amount in respect of any loss of earnings necessarily suffered, or any additional expenses (other than expenses on account of travelling or subsistence) necessarily suffered or incurred by him for the purpose of enabling him to perform that duty.

(5) [Repealed.]

(6) A member of a parish or community council shall not be entitled to any payment under this section in respect of the

performance as such a member of an approved duty within the parish or community or, in the case of a parish or community grouped under a common parish or community council, the area of the group.

Right to opt for financial loss allowance

173A.—(1) If a councillor gives notice in writing to the parish or community council of which he is a member that he wishes to receive financial loss allowance, he shall be entitled, subject to and in accordance with the following provisions of this section, to receive that allowance instead of any payment by way of attendance allowance to which he would otherwise to be entitled.

(2) A notice under this section is referred to in this section as a "financial loss allowance notice".

(3) If a councillor gives a financial loss allowance notice to the parish or community council, not later than the end of the period of one month beginning with the day of his election as a member of the council, then, subject to subsection (4A) below, he shall be entitled to received financial loss allowance for the performance of any approved duty since his election, whether performed before or after the giving of the notice.

(4) If a councillor gives a financial loss allowance notice to the parish or community council otherwise than in accordance with subsection (3) above, then, subject to subsection (4A) below, he shall be entitled to receive financial loss allowance for the performance of any approved duty after the end of the period of one month beginning with the day on which the notice is given.

(4A) If a councillor who has given a parish or community council a financial loss allowance notice gives them notice in writing that he withdraws that notice, it shall not have effect in relation to any duty performed after the day on which the notice of withdrawal is given.

Travelling allowance and subsistence allowance

174.—(1)   Subject to subsections (2) and (3) below, a member of a body to which this section applies shall be entitled to receive payments by way of travelling allowance or subsistence allowance where expenditure on travelling (whether inside or outside the United Kingdom) or, as the case may be, on subsistence is necessarily incurred by him for the purpose of enabling him to perform any approved duty as a member of that body, being payments at rates determined by that body, but not exceeding, in the case of travel or subsistence for the purpose of an approved duty within the United Kingdom, such rates as may be specified by the Secretary of State.

(2)   A member of a parish or community council shall not be entitled to any payment under this section in respect of the performance as such a member of an approved duty within the parish or community or, in the case of a parish or community grouped under a common parish or community council, the area of the group.

(3)   [Repealed.]

Allowances for attending conferences and meetings

175.—(1)   The following bodies, that is to say—

(a)   any local authority;

(b)   any other body to which this section applies and which has power by virtue of any enactment to send representatives to any conference or meeting to which this section applies;

may pay any such member of the authority or other body attending any such conference or meeting such allowances in the nature of an attendance allowance and an allowance for travelling and subsistence as they think fit.

(1A)   Payments made under subsection (1) above shall be of such reasonable amounts as the body in question may determine in a particular case or class of case but shall not exceed—

(a) in the case of payments of an allowance in the nature of an attendance allowance, such amounts as may be specified in or determined under regulations made by the Secretary of State; and

(b) in the case of payments of an allowance in the nature of an allowance for travel or subsistence in respect of a conference or meeting held in the United Kingdom, such amounts as may be specified under s.174 above for the corresponding allowance under that section;

and regulations made by the Secretary of State may make it a condition of any payment mentioned in paragraph (a) above that, in the financial year to which the payment would relate, the aggregate amount which the body in question has paid or is already liable to pay in respect of any prescribed allowance or allowances does not exceed such maximum amount as may be specified in or determined under the regulations.

(2) Where a body mentioned in subsection (1)(b) above has power under any enactment other than this Act or any instrument under such an enactment to pay expenses incurred in attending a conference or meeting to which this section applies, the amount payable under that enactment or instrument shall not exceed the amount which would be payable in respect of the attendance under that subsection.

(3) In relation to a local authority this section applies to a conference or meeting held inside or outside the United Kingdom and convened by any person or body (other than a person or body convening it in the course of a trade or business or a body the objects of which are wholly or partly political) for the purpose of discussing matters which in their opinion relate to the interests of their area or any part of it or the interests of the inhabitants of their area or any part of it.

(3A) [Repealed.]

(3B) In relation to ... any body which is a joint board, joint authority or other combined body all the members of which are representatives of local authorities this section applies to a conference or meeting held and convened as mentioned in subsection (3) above for the purpose of discussing matters which in the body's opinion relate—

(a) to the functions of the body; or

(b) to any functions of local authorities in which the body has an interest.

(4) In relation to any other body to which this section applies this section applies to a conference or meeting convened by one or more such bodies or by an association of such bodies.

Payment of expenses of official and courtesy visits, etc.

176.—(1) Subject to subsection (2) below, a local authority may—

(a) defray any travelling or other expenses reasonably incurred by or on behalf of any members in making official and courtesy visits, whether inside or outside the United Kingdom, on behalf of the authority;

(b) defray any expenses incurred in the reception and entertainment by way of official courtesy of distinguished persons visiting the area of the authority and persons representative of or connected with local government or other public services whether inside or outside the United Kingdom and in supply of information to any such persons.

(2) In the case of a visit within the United Kingdom, the amount defrayed under this section by a local authority in respect of the expenses of any member of the authority in making a visit within the United Kingdom shall not exceed the payments which he would have been entitled to receive by

way of travelling allowance or subsistence allowance under section 174 above if the making of the visit had been an approved duty of that member.

(3) In this section "local authority" includes a joint authority...

Provisions supplementary to sections 173 to 176

177.—(1) Sections 174 and 175 above apply—

(a) to the bodies specified in section 21(1) of the Local Government and Housing Act 1989, except—

    (i) the Common Council;

    (ii) a body established pursuant to an order under section 67 of the Local Government Act 1985 (successors to residuary bodies); and

    (iii) without prejudice to section 265 below, the Council of the Isles of Scilly;

(b) to any prescribed body on which a body to which those sections apply by virtue of paragraph (a) above is represented; and

(c) to any parish or community council.

(1A) [Omitted.]

(2) In sections 173 to 176 above 'approved duty', in relation to a member of a body, means such duties as may be specified in or determined under regulations made by the Secretary of State.

(3) For the purposes of sections 173 to 176 above a member of a committee or sub-committee of a local authority or other body mentioned in subsection (1) above shall be deemed to be a member of that body.

(4) Section 94(5) above shall apply in relation to a member of any body mentioned in subsection (1) above to

whom it would not otherwise apply as it applies in relation to a member of a local authority; and no other enactment or instrument shall prevent a member of any such body from taking part in the consideration or determination of any allowance or other payment under any of the provisions of sections 173 to 176 above or under any scheme made by virtue of section 18 of the Local Government and Housing Act 1989.

178.—(1) The Secretary of State may make regulations as to the manner in which sections 173 to 176 above are to be administered, and in particular, and without prejudice to the generality of the foregoing provision, may make regulations—

(a) providing for the avoidance of duplication in payments under those sections, or between payments under any of those sections and any other Act, and for the determination of the body or bodies by whom any payments under those sections are to be made, and where such payments are to be made by more than one body, for the apportionment between those bodies of the sums payable;

(b) specifying the forms to be used and the particulars to be provided for the purpose of claiming payments under those sections;

(c) providing for the publication by a body to which sections 173 to 175 above apply, in the minutes of that body or otherwise, of details of such payments.

(2) A statutory instrument containing regulations under section 173 or 177 above or this section shall be subject to annulment in pursuance of a resolution of either House of Parliament.

(4) THE LOCAL AUTHORITIES (MEMBERS' ALLOWANCES) REGULATIONS 1991

S.I. 1991 No. 351

(as amended by S.I. 1995 No. 553 and S.I. 1996 No. 469 and S.I. 2000 No. 622, 623 (in relation to England); S.I. 2000 No. 1553, 2492 (in relation to Wales)

Made	*28th February 1991*
Laid before Parliament	*28th February 1991*

Coming into force
Regulations 1, 2 and 4 to 15	*1st March 1991*
Remainder	*1st April 1991*

ARRANGEMENT OF REGULATIONS

PART I
General

PART II
Schemes for Members' Allowances

PART III
Schemes — Financial Restrictions

PART IV
Schemes — Further Provision

13. Amount of allowances etc.
14. Elections
15. Claims and payments

PART V
Other Allowances

16. Definition of "approved duty"
17. Financial restrictions — allowances under section 175 of the 1972 Act
18. Financial restrictions — allowances under section 173 of the 1972 Act
19. Bodies prescribed under section 177(1)

PART VI
Administrative Arrangements

20.–22. Avoidance of duplication
23.–25. Paying Allowances
26. Records of allowances
26A. Publicity

PART VII
Revocations and Savings

27.   Revocations and savings

SCHEDULE
Determination of the standard maximum.

The Secretary of State for the Environment, as respects England, and the Secretary of State for Wales, as respects Wales, in exercise of the powers conferred upon them by sections 173, 175(1A), 177(1)(b) and (f), 177(2), 178(1) and 270(1) of the Local Government Act 1972, sections 18 and 190(1) of the Local Government and Housing Act 1989 and of all other powers enabling them in that behalf, hereby make the following Regulations:—

PART I

GENERAL

Citation and commencement

1.—(1) These Regulations may be cited as the Local Authorities (Members' Allowances) Regulations 1991.

(2) This Part (except for regulation 3) and Parts II to IV of these Regulations shall come into force on 1st March 1991.

(3) The remainder of these Regulations shall come into force on 1st April 1991.

Interpretation

2. In these Regulations—

"the 1972 Act" means the Local Government Act 1972;

"the 1985 Act" means the Local Government Act 1985;

"the 1989 Act" means the Local Government and Housing Act 1989;

"joint authority" means an authority established under Part IV of the 1985 Act;

"year" means the 12 months ending with 31st March.

Prescribed bodies

3. The following bodies (being bodies on which a body to which sections 174 and 175 of the 1972 Act apply by virtue of section 177(1)(a) of that Act is represented) are prescribed pursuant to section 177(1)(b) of the 1972 Act—

(a) a joint committee of two or more local authorities, whether appointed or established under Part VI of that Act or any other enactment;

(b) a joint education committee established under paragraph 3 of Part II of Schedule 1 to the Education Act 1944; and

(c) the Cheshire Brine Subsidence Compensation Board;

and for the purposes of sections 174 and 175 of the 1972 Act a National Park authority shall be treated as a local authority within the meaning of paragraph (a) above.

Members of authorities to be treated as councillors

4. For the purposes of section 18 of the 1989 Act, a member of (a) a joint authority who is appointed to that authority by a metropolitan district council, a London borough council, Northumberland County Council or the Common Council of the City of London (b) the London Fire and Emergency Planning Authority who is appointed to that authority by the Mayor on the nomination of the London borough councils acting jointly shall be treated as if he were a councillor, and references in Parts II to IV to councillors shall be construed accordingly.

PART II
SCHEMES FOR MEMBERS' ALLOWANCES

Application of Part II and interpretation

5.—(1) This Part applies—

(a) in England, to a county, district or London borough council, and the Council of the Isles of Scilly;

(b) in Wales, to a county or county borough council;

(c) to any joint authority; and

(d) to any National Park authority;[1]

---

[1]   Each National Park authority established for a National Park in England shall as soon as practicable after the day on which it is established make a scheme in accordance with the principal regulations for the payment of allowances for the period beginning on that day and ending with the end of the year in which that day falls, and for subsequent years.

and in relation to a National Park authority references in this Part to a councillor shall (subject to paragraph (2)(b)) be construed as references to a member of that authority appointed by a principal council or the Secretary of State.

(2) For the purposes of this Part—

(a) members of an authority are to be treated as divided into political groups if they are so treated for the purposes of section 15 (political balance on committees etc.) of the 1989 Act; and "political group" shall be construed accordingly;

(b) the term of office of a councillor who is a member of an authority specified in paragraph (1) other than a joint authority or a National Park authority shall begin on the date on which he makes a declaration of acceptance of that office under section 83(1) of the 1972 Act.

Allowance schemes

6.—(1) Before 1st April 1991 each authority shall make a scheme in accordance with these Regulations for the payment of allowances in respect of the year commencing on that date and subsequent years.

(2) When a scheme is revoked in accordance with regulation 7(1), an authority shall before the revocation takes effect make a further scheme for the period beginning with the date on which the revocation takes effect.

Amendment of schemes

7.—(1) A scheme under this Part may be amended at any time but may only be revoked with effect from the beginning of a year.

(2) Where an amendment is to be made which affects an allowance payable for the year in which the amendment is

made, the scheme shall provide—

- (a) if the amendment affects such an allowance as is mentioned in regulation 8 or 9, that in relation to each of the periods—

    - (i) beginning with the year and ending with the day before that on which the first amendment in that year takes effect, and

    - (ii) beginning with the day on which an amendment takes effect and ending with the day before that on which the next amendment takes effect, or (if none) with the year,

    the entitlement to such an allowance shall be to payment of such part of the amount of the allowance under the scheme as it has effect during the relevant period as bears to the whole the same proportion as the number of days in the period bears to the number of days in the year;

- (b) if the amendment affects such an allowance as is mentioned in regulation 10, that the entitlement to such an allowance shall be to payment of the amount of the allowance under the scheme as it has effect when the duty is carried out.

Basic allowances

8.—(1) A scheme made under this Part shall provide for the payment for each year to which the scheme relates of an allowance ("basic allowance") to each member of the authority who is a councillor; and the amount of such allowance shall be the same for each such member.

(2) The scheme shall provide that, where the term of office of a member begins or ends otherwise than at the beginning or end of a year, his entitlement shall be to payment of such part of the basic allowance as bears to the whole the

same proportion as the number of days during which his term of office as member and councillor subsists bears to the number of days in that year.

(3) Where a scheme is amended as mentioned in paragraph (2) of regulation 7 and the term of office of a member who is a councillor does not subsist throughout the whole of a period mentioned in sub-paragraph (a) of that paragraph, the scheme shall provide that the entitlement of any such member under this regulation shall be to payment of such part of the basic allowance referable to each such period (ascertained in accordance with that sub-paragraph) as bears to the whole the same proportion as the number of days during which his term of office as member and councillor subsists in that period bears to the number of days in the period.

Special responsibility allowances

9.—(1) A scheme made under this Part may provide, in accordance with paragraph (2), for the payment for each year to which that scheme relates of an allowance ("special responsibility allowance") to such members of the authority who are councillors as have such special responsibilities in relation to the authority as are specified in the scheme and are within one or ore of the following categories—

(a) acting as leader or deputy leader of a political group within the authority;

(b) presiding at meetings of a committee or a sub-committee of the authority, or a joint committee of the authority and one or more other authorities, or a sub-committee of such a joint committee;

(c) representing the authority at meetings of, or arranged by, any other body;

(d) membership of a committee or a sub-committee of

the authority which meets with exceptional frequency or for exceptionally long periods;

(e) acting as the spokesman of a political group on a committee or sub-committee of the authority;

(f) such other activities in relation to the discharge of the authority's functions as require of the member an amount of time and effort equal to or greater than would be required of him by any one of the activities mentioned in sub-paragraphs (a) to (e) (whether or not that activity is specified in the scheme).

(2) Any scheme making such provision as is mentioned in paragraph (1) shall—

(a) specify the amount of each special responsibility allowance, which need not be the same; and

(b) provide that, where—

(i) members of an authority are divided into at least two groups constituted in accordance with regulation 8 of the Local Government (Committees and Political Groups) Regulations 1990, and

(ii) either a majority of members of the authority, or half of such members and the chairman of the authority, belong to the same political group ("the controlling group"),

a special responsibility allowance shall be paid to at least one person who is not a member of the controlling group and has special responsibilities described in paragraph (1)(a) or (e); and

(c) provide that, where a member does not have throughout a year any such special responsibilities as entitle him to a special responsibility allowance, his entitlement shall be to payment of such part of that allowance as bears to the whole the same proportion as the number of days during which he has such special responsibilities bears to the number of days in that year; and

(d) provide that, where a scheme is amended as mentioned in paragraph (2) of regulation 7 and a member does not have throughout the whole of any period mentioned in sub-paragraph (a) of that paragraph any such special responsibilities as entitle him to a special responsibility allowance, his entitlement shall be to payment of such part of the allowance referable to each such period (ascertained in accordance with that sub-paragraph) as bears to the whole the same proportion as the number of days in that period during which he has such special responsibilities bears to the number of days in the period.

Attendance allowances

10.—(1) Subject to paragraph (2), a scheme made under this Part may provide for the payment to each member of the authority who is a councillor of an allowance ("attendance allowance") in respect of—

(a) the carrying out of such of the duties referred to in paragraph (3) or (3A) and not excluded by paragraph (4) as may be specified in the scheme; and

(b) the time spent in travelling to and from the location at which any such duty so specified is performed.

(2) A scheme made by the council of a metropolitan district or a London borough or the county of Northumberland shall not provide for the payment of an attendance allowance in respect of any duty carried out by a member of the authority who is a councillor in his capacity as that authority's representative on a joint authority.

(2A) A scheme made by the council for a principal area shall not provide for the payment of an attendance allowance in respect of any duty carried out by a member of the authority who is a councillor in his capacity as a member of a National Park authority appointed by that authority.

(3) The duties referred to in this paragraph are attendance at—

(a) a meeting of the authority or of any committee or sub-committee of the authority, or of any other body to which the authority makes appointments or nominations, or of any committee or sub-committee of such a body;

(b) any other meeting the holding of which is authorised by the authority, or a committee or sub-committee of the authority, or a joint committee of the authority and one or more other authorities, or a sub-committee of such a joint committee, provided that—

(i) where the authority is divided into two or more political groups, it is a meeting to which members of at least two such groups have been invited, or

(ii) if the authority is not so divided, it is a meeting to which at least two members of the authority have been invited;

(c) a meeting of any association of authorities of which the authority is a member.

(3A) The duties referred to in this paragraph are duties undertaken on behalf of the authority—

(a) in pursuance of any standing order requiring a member or members to be present while tender documents are opened;

(b) in connection with the discharge of any function of the authority conferred by or under any enactment and empowering or requiring the authority to inspect or authorise the inspection of premises; or

(c) in connection with arrangements made by the authority for the attendance of pupils at a school approved for the purposes of section 188 (special schools) of the Education Act 1993.

(4) The duties excluded by this paragraph are those in respect of which the member receives remuneration otherwise than under a scheme.

(5) The amount of the attendance allowance shall be specified in the scheme and may vary according to the time of day and the duration of the duty; but shall be the same for all members of the authority entitled to the allowance in respect of a duty of any description at the same time of day and of the same duration.

(6) The scheme shall provide that a member shall not be entitled to payment of an attendance allowance—

(a) in respect of his attendance at any conference or meeting in relation to which he is entitled to a payment in the nature of an attendance allowance under section 175 of the 1972 Act; or

(b) if such payment would be contrary to a provision made by or under any enactment.

(7) The scheme may provide that a member shall not be entitled to payment of more than one attendance allowance in respect of any period of 24 hours beginning at such time as the authority may determine.

PART III
SCHEMES — FINANCIAL RESTRICTIONS

Application of Part III and interpretation

11. *[Revoked.]*

Financial restrictions

12. *[Revoked.]*

PART IV

SCHEMES — FURTHER PROVISION

Amount of allowances etc

13. A scheme under Part II shall specify in respect of any year to which it relates—

(a) the amount of the entitlement by way of basic allowance;

(b) the amount of the entitlement by way of special responsibility allowance; and where different amounts apply to different responsibilities, the amount applicable to each;

(c) the rates applicable to payments by way of attendance allowance (where the scheme provides for that allowance).

Elections

14. A scheme under Part II shall provide that a member may, by notice in writing given to the proper officer of the authority, elect to forgo any part of his entitlement to an allowance under the scheme.

Claims and payments

15.—(1) A scheme under Part II shall provide that a claim for an attendance allowance under the scheme shall be made within two months of the date on which the duty in respect of which the entitlement to the allowance arises is carried out.

(2) Nothing in paragraph (1) shall prevent an authority from making a payment where the allowance is not claimed within the period specified in the scheme.

(3) A scheme under Part II may provide for payments of allowances to be made at such times as may be specified in it, and different times may be specified for different allowances.

PART V
OTHER ALLOWANCES

Definition of "approved duty"

16. For the purposes of sections 173 to 176 of the 1972 Act "approved duty" means—

(a) any of the duties specified in regulation 10(3)(a) to (c); and

(b) any other duty approved by the body, or any duty of a class so approved, for the purpose of, or in connection with, the discharge of the functions of the body, or of any of its committees or sub-committees.

Financial restrictions — allowances under section 175 of the 1972 Act

17.—(1) *[Revoked.]*

(2) Any payment of an allowance under section 175 of the 1972 Act in the nature of an attendance allowance (other than such a payment by a body to which Part II applies to a member who is a councillor) shall not exceed £30.39 for any period not exceeding 24 hours; and for this purpose a period of 24 hours shall begin at 3am.

Financial restrictions — allowances under section 173 of the 1972 Act

18.—(1) The amount prescribed for the purpose of section 173(1) of the 1972 Act (attendance allowance) is £30.39 for any period not exceeding 24 hours; and for this purpose a period of 24 hours shall begin at 3am.

(2) The amount prescribed for the purposes of sections

173(4) of the 1972 Act (financial loss allowance) is—

- (a) for a period not exceeding 4 hours, £27.65;

- (b) for a period exceeding 4 hours but not exceeding 24 hours, £55.31;

- (c) for a period exceeding 24 hours, the aggregate of £55.31 and such amount specified in sub-paragraph (a) or (b) as is appropriate to the number of hours by which the period exceeds 24 hours.

Bodies prescribed under section 177(1)

19. The following bodies are prescribed in accordance with section 177(1)(f) of the 1972 Act—

- (a) the Peak Park Joint Planning Board;

- (b) the Lake District Special Planning Board;

- (c) a combined police authority;

- (d) a joint education committee established under paragraph 3 of Part II of Schedule 1 to the Education Act 1944, of which the members are not all representatives of local authorities; and

- (e) the Cheshire Brine Subsidence Compensation Board.

PART VI
ADMINISTRATIVE ARRANGEMENTS

Avoidance of duplication

20. A claim for an attendance allowance under the scheme or an allowance under any provision in sections 173 to 176 of the 1972 Act shall include, or be accompanied by, a statement signed by the claimant that he has not made and will not make any other claim in respect of the matter to which his claim relates.

21. No payment shall be made to a person under any provision of sections 173 to 176 of the 1972 Act in respect of a matter as regards which a payment has been made to him pursuant to any provision of a scheme under Part II.

22.—(1) A person who, in a period mentioned in regulation 18,—

(a) performs an approved duty or approved duties as a member of more than one body;

(b) performs two or more approved duties for the same body; or

(c) is entitled to an allowance under section 173 of the 1972 Act and to a payment of a comparable allowance under any other enactment

shall not be entitled to payments under that section which in total exceed the amount prescribed by regulation 18 for that period.

(2) A body paying an allowance under section 173 of the 1972 Act to a person for an approved duty as described in paragraph (1) may reduce the amount of that allowance by the amount of any other allowance under section 173 or any comparable allowance under any enactment paid by another body.

Paying allowances

23. A payment under section 173 or 174 of the 1972 Act shall be made by the body for which the relevant approved duty was performed, except as provided for in regulations 24 and 25.

24. Where a member of a body, who has been appointed by that body to some other body, performs an approved duty for that other body, and that other body is—

(a) a joint committee of two or more local authorities,

whether appointed or established under Part VI of the 1972 Act or any other enactment;

(b) a joint board or other combined body, all the members of which are representatives of local authorities; or

(c) a body mentioned in regulation 19

either body may make a payment under section 173 or 174 of the 1972 Act and for the purposes of this regulation a National Park authority shall be treated as a local authority within the meaning of paragraph (a) and as a combined body all the members of which are representatives of local authorities within the meaning of paragraph (b).

25. An allowance payable under section 173(4) or 174 of the 1972 Act to a member of an appeal committee constituted under paragraph 2 or 3 of Schedule 2 to the Education Act 1980 shall be paid by the local education authority which maintains the school or schools in relation to which the committee is constituted.

Records of allowances

26.—(1) Every authority shall keep a record of the payments made by it in accordance with any scheme made pursuant to these Regulations.

(2) Every authority, body or council shall keep a record of the payments made by it by virtue of any provision of sections 173 to 176 of the 1972 Act.

(3) A record kept pursuant to either of the preceding paragraphs shall specify the name of the recipient and the amount and nature of each payment.

(4) Any such record shall be available, at all reasonable times, for inspection (free of charge)—

(a) where it is kept by a local authority within the meaning of section 270(1) of the 1972 Act or a joint authority, by any local government elector (within the meaning of that section) for the area of that authority;

(b) where it is kept by any other body, by any such local government elector of any such local authority in whose area the body operates.

(5) A person entitled to inspect a record under paragraph (4) may make a copy of any part of it.

Publicity

26A.—(1) Every authority shall, as soon as practicable after the making or amendment of any scheme made pursuant to these Regulations, make arrangements for its publication within the authority's area.

(2) As soon as practicable after the end of a year to which a scheme relates, every authority shall make arrangements for the publication within the authority's area of the total sum paid by it in that year under the scheme to each member in respect of each of the following, namely, basic allowance, special responsibility allowance and attendance allowance.

PART VII

REVOCATIONS AND SAVINGS

Revocations and savings

27.—(1) Subject to paragraph (2), the Local Government (Allowances) Regulations 1986, the Local Government (Allowances) (Amendment) Regulations 1987, the Local Government (Allowances) (Amendment) Regulations 1988 and the Local Government (Allowances) (Amendment) Regulations 1989 are revoked.

(2) The Regulations mentioned in paragraph (1) shall continue to have effect without prejudice to section 16 of the Interpretation Act 1978, in relation to claims made for allowances or other payments in respect of duties performed before 1st April 1991.

(5) THE LOCAL AUTHORITIES (MEMBERS' ALLOWANCES) (ENGLAND) REGULATIONS 2001
S.I. 2001 No. 1280

Made	*1st April 2001*
Laid before Parliament	*2nd April 2001*
Coming into force	*4th May 2001*

The Secretary of State for the Environment, Transport and the Regions in exercise of the powers conferred on him by section 177(2) of the Local Government Act 1972, and sections 18 and 190(1) of the Local Government and Housing Act 1989, and of all other powers enabling him in that behalf, hereby makes the following Regulations:—

Citation, commencement and extent

1.—(1)   These Regulations may be cited as the Local Authorities (Members' Allowances) (England) Regulations 2001 and shall come into force on 4th May 2001.

(2)   These Regulations extend to England only.

Interpretation

2.   In these Regulations—

"the 1972 Act" means the Local Government Act 1972;

"the 1991 Regulations" means the Local Authorities (Members' Allowances) Regulations 1991;

"allowance scheme" means a scheme for allowances made pursuant to Part II of the 1991 Regulations;

"alternative arrangements" has the same meaning as in Part II of the Local Government Act 2000;

"basic allowance" has the same meaning as in regulation 8 of the 1991 Regulations;

"executive" has the same meaning as in Part II of the Local Government Act 2000;

"executive arrangements" has the same meaning as in Part II of the Local Government Act 2000;

"independent remuneration panel" means a panel or joint panel established under regulation 4 of these Regulations;

"political group" shall be construed in accordance with section 15 of the Local Government and Housing Act 1989;

"special responsibility allowance" has the same meaning as in regulation 9 of the 1991 Regulations; and

"the Association of London Government" means the body known by that name and established in April 2000 as a joint committee by all the London borough councils and the Corporation of the City of London.

Duty to have regard to recommendations

3.   Before they make or amend an allowance scheme in accordance with regulation 7 of these Regulations or regulation 6 or 7 of the 1991 Regulations, a district, county or London borough council shall have regard to the recommendations which have been made in relation to them by an independent remuneration panel.

Independent remuneration panels

4.—(1)   An independent remuneration panel may be established—

(a) by a district, county or London borough council and shall exercise the functions specified in regulation 5 in respect of that authority;

(b) jointly by any district, county or London borough council and shall exercise the functions specified in regulation 5 in respect of the authorities which established it; or

(c) by the Association of London Government, and shall exercise the functions specified in regulation 5 in respect of any London borough councils.

(2) An independent remuneration panel shall consist of at least three members none of whom may also be a member of a district, county or London borough council.

(3) A person may not be a member of an independent remuneration panel if he is disqualified from being or becoming a member of a district, county or London borough council.

(4) A district, county or London borough council may pay the expenses incurred by an independent remuneration panel established under paragraph (1)(a) or (b) in carrying out its functions and may pay the members of the panel such allowances or expenses as the district, county or London borough council for which it exercises functions may determine.

(5) The Association of London Government may pay the expenses incurred by an independent remuneration panel established under paragraph (1)(c) in carrying out its functions and may pay the members of the panel such allowances or expenses as the Association of London Government may determine.

Recommendations of panels

5.—(1) An independent remuneration panel shall produce a report in relation to the members of each district, county or London borough council in respect of which it exercises functions making recommendations—

(a) as to the amount of basic allowance which should be payable to such members;

(b) as to the duties in respect of which such members should receive a special responsibility allowance and as to the amount of such an allowance; and

(c) as to whether the allowance scheme of such district,

county or London borough council should include allowances in respect of the expenses of arranging for the care of children or dependants of such members in accordance with regulation 8, and as to the amount of such allowances.

(2) A copy of a report made under paragraph (1) shall be sent to each district, county and London borough council in respect of which recommendations have been made.

(3) An independent remuneration panel may make different recommendations in relation to each of the authorities for which it exercises functions.

Publicity for recommendations of panels

6.—(1)   Where a district, county or London borough council receives a copy of a report made to them by an independent remuneration panel in accordance with regulation 5(1), they shall, as soon as reasonably practicable after receiving the report—

- (a) ensure that copies of that report are available for inspection by members of the public at the principal office of the authority, at all reasonable hours, and

- (b) publish in one or more newspapers circulating in their area, a notice which—

  - (i) states that they have received recommendations from an independent remuneration panel in respect of their allowance scheme;

  - (ii) describes the main features of that panel's recommendations and specifies the recommended amounts of each allowance mentioned in its report in respect of that authority;

  - (iii) states that copies of the panel's report are available at the principal office of the authority for inspection by members of the public at such times as may be specified by the authority in the notice; and

(iv) specifies the address of the principal office of the authority at which such copies are made available.

(2) A district, county or London borough council shall supply a copy of a report sent to them by an independent remuneration panel in accordance with regulation 5(1) to any person who requests a copy and who pays to the authority such reasonable fee as the authority may determine.

Transitional provision for revocation of allowance schemes

7.—(1) Where an independent remuneration panel has produced a report in accordance with regulation 5, a district, county or London borough council may, notwithstanding regulation 7(1) of the 1991 Regulations, revoke an allowance scheme—

(a) once at any time before 1st April 2002 in consequence of the coming into force of section 18(1A) of the Local Government and Housing Act 1989; and

(b) at any time once that council has begun to operate—

(i) executive arrangements, including where they are being operated in place of existing alternative arrangements;

(ii) alternative arrangements, including where they are being operated in place of existing executive arrangements; or

(iii) different executive arrangements which involve an executive which takes a different form.

(2) When a scheme is revoked in accordance with paragraph (1) the district, county or London borough council shall before the revocation takes effect make a further scheme for the period beginning with the date on which the revocation takes effect.

(3) A further scheme made under paragraph (2) shall include provision for an appropriate adjustment in respect of any basic allowance or special responsibility allowance which—

(a) has already been paid under the previous scheme in respect of the remainder of the year from which the further scheme has effect; or

(b) is to be paid in respect of any part of the year during which the previous scheme had effect.

Childcare and dependants carers' allowances

8.   An allowance scheme may include provision for the payment to members of district, county or London borough councils of allowances in respect of such expenses of arranging for the care of their children or dependants as are necessarily incurred in—

(a) the attendance at a meeting of the authority or of any committee or sub-committee of the authority, or of any other body to which the authority make appointments or nominations, or of any committee or sub-committee of such a body;

(b) the attendance at any other meeting, the holding of which is authorised by the authority, or a committee or sub-committee of the authority, or a joint committee of the authority and one or more local authority within the meaning of section 270(1) of the 1972 Act, or a sub-committee of such a joint committee provided that—

   (i) where the authority are divided into two or more political groups, it is a meeting to which members of at least two such groups have been invited; or

   (ii) if the authority are not so divided, it is a meeting to which at least two members of the authority have been invited;

(c) the attendance at a meeting of any association of

authorities of which the authority are a member;

(d) the attendance at a meeting of the executive or a meeting of any of its committees, where the authority are operating executive arrangements;

(e) the performance of any duty in pursuance of any standing order made under section 135 of the 1972 Act requiring a member or members to be present while tender documents are opened;

(f) the performance of any duty in connection with the discharge of any function of the authority conferred by or under any enactment and empowering or requiring the authority to inspect or authorise the inspection of premises; and

(g) the performance of any duty in connection with arrangements made by the authority for the attendance of pupils at school approved for the purposes of section 342 (special schools) of the Education Act 1996.

Publicity for allowance schemes

9.—(1) Regulation 26A of the 1991 Regulations shall not apply to district, county or London borough councils.

(2) After regulation 26A (2) of the 1991 Regulations there shall be inserted—

"(3) This regulation is subject to regulation 9 of the Local Authorities (Members' Allowances) (England) Regulations 2001."

(3) A district, county or London borough council shall, as soon as reasonably practicable after the making or amendment of an allowance scheme make arrangements for its publication by—

(a) ensuring that copies of the scheme are available for inspection by members of the public at the principal office of the authority, at all reasonable hours; and

(b) publishing in one or more newspapers circulating in their area, a notice which—

(i) states that the authority have made or amended a scheme for allowances and specifies the period of time for which the scheme has effect;

(ii) describes the main features of the scheme and specifies the amounts of each allowance mentioned in that scheme;

(iii) states that in making or amending the scheme, the authority complied with their functions in accordance with regulation 3 of these regulations in having regard to the recommendations of an independent remuneration panel;

(iv) describes the main features of that panel's recommendations and specifies the recommended amounts of each allowance mentioned in its report in respect of that authority;

(v) states that copies of the scheme are available at the principal office of the authority for inspection by members of the public at such times as may be specified by the authority in the notice; and

(vi) specifies the address of the principal office of the authority at which such copies are made available.

(4) A district, county or London borough council shall supply a copy of the scheme to any person who requests a copy and who pays to the authority such reasonable fee as the authority may determine.

(5) As soon as reasonably practicable after the end of a year to which a scheme relates, a district, county or London borough council shall make arrangements for the publication within the authority's area of the total sum paid by them in the year under the scheme to each member in respect of each of the following—

(a) basic allowance;

(b) special responsibility allowance;

(c) attendance allowance; and

(d) allowances in respect of arranging for the care of children or dependants in accordance with regulation 8.

Special responsibility allowances

10. In regulation 9 (1) (special responsibility allowance) of the 1991 Regulations, after paragraph (a) there is inserted—

"(aa) membership of an executive where the authority are operating executive arrangements within the meaning of Part II of the Local Government Act 2000;"

Definition of "approved duty"

11.—(1) For regulation 16 (definition of "approved duty") of the 1991 Regulations, there shall be substituted—

"16.—(1) For the purposes of section 173 to 176 of the 1972 Act "approved duty" means—

(a) any of the duties specified in regulation 10(3) (a) to (c) and (3A); and

(b) any other duty approved by the body, or any duty of a class so approved, for the purpose of, or in connection with, the discharge of the functions of the body, or of any of its committees or sub-committees.

(2) For the purposes of section 174 of the 1972 Act "approved duty" includes, in addition to the duties specified in paragraph (1) of this regulation, any duty for the purpose of, or in connection with, the discharge of the functions of an executive, where the authority are operating executive arrangements within the meaning of Part II of the Local Government Act 2000."

(6) RATES OF TRAVELLING AND SUBSISTENCE ALLOWANCES

(The rates are those in force on 1st January 2002)

PART 1
RATES OF TRAVELLING ALLOWANCES AND PROVISIONS RELATING THERETO

1.—(1) The rate of travel by public transport shall not exceed the amount of the ordinary fare or any available cheap fare, and where more than one class of fare is available the rate shall be determined, in the case of travel by ship by reference to first class fares, and in any other case by reference to second class fares unless the body determines either generally or specifically, that first class fares shall be substituted.

(2) The rate specified in the proceeding sub-paragraph may be increased by supplementary allowances not exceeding expenditure actually incurred:

(a) on Pullman Car or similar supplements, reservation of seats and deposit or porterage of luggage; and

(b) on sleeping accommodation engaged by the member for an overnight journey, subject, however, to reduction by one-third of any subsistence allowance payable to him/her for that night.

2.—(1) The rate for travel by a member's own solo motor cycle, or one provided for his/her use, shall not exceed:

(a) for the use of a solo motor cycle of cylinder capacity not exceeding 150cc, 8.5 pence per mile;

(b) for use of a solo motor cycle of cylinder capacity exceeding 150cc. but not exceeding 500cc, 12.3 pence per mile;

(c) for use of a solo motor cycle of cylinder capacity exceeding 500cc, 16.5 pence per mile.

(2) The rate for travel by a member's own private motor vehicle, or one belonging to a member of his/her family or otherwise provided for his/her use, other than a solo motor cycle, shall not exceed—

(a) for the use of a motor vehicle of cylinder capacity

  (i)   not exceeding 999cc, 34.6 pence per mile;

  (ii) exceeding 999cc but not exceeding 1199cc, 39.5 pence per mile;

  (iii) exceeding 1199cc, 48.5 pence per mile.

(3) The rates specified in sub-paragraphs (1) and (2) may be increased—

(a) in respect of the carriage of passengers, not exceeding 4, to whom a travelling allowance would otherwise be payable under any enactment, by not more than 3.0 pence a mile for the first passenger and 2.0 pence per mile for the second and subsequent passengers;

(b) by not more than the amount of any expenditure incurred on tolls, ferries or parking fees, including overnight garaging.

(4) For the purposes of this paragraph the cylinder capacity shall be that entered in the vehicle registration book or document by the Secretary of State under the Vehicles (Excise) Act 1971.

3. The rate of travel by taxi-cab or cab shall not exceed:

(a) in cases of urgency or where no public transport is reasonably available, the amount of the actual fare and any reasonable gratuity paid; and

(b) in any other case, the amount of the fare for travel by appropriate public transport.

4. The rate of travel by a hired motor vehicle other than a taxi-cab shall not exceed the rate which would have been

applicable had the vehicle belonged to the member who hired it—

Provided that where the body so approves the rate may be increased to an amount not exceeding the actual cost of hiring.

5. The rate of travel by air shall not exceed the rate applicable to travel by appropriate alternative means of transport together with an allowance equivalent to the amount of any saving in attendance allowance or financial loss allowance, and subsistence allowance consequent on travel by air—

Provided that where the body resolves, either generally or specifically, that the saving in time is so substantial as to justify payment of the fare for travel by air, there may be paid an amount not exceeding:

(a) the ordinary fare or any available cheap fare for travel by regular air service, or

(b) where no such service is available or in case of urgency, the fare actually paid by the member.

PART 2
RATES OF SUBSISTENCE ALLOWANCE, AND PROVISIONS RELATING THERETO

1.—(1) The rate of subsistence allowance shall not exceed:

(a) in the case of an absence, not involving an absence overnight, from the usual place of residence;

(i) of more than 4 hours, or where the authority permits, a lesser period, before 11am, (breakfast allowance), £4.92;

(ii) of more than 4 hours, or where the authority permits, a lesser period, including the period between 12 noon and 2 pm, (lunch allowance), £6.77;

(iii) of more than 4 hours, or where the authority permits, a lesser period, including the period 3 pm to 6 pm, (tea allowance), £2.67;

(iv) of more than 4 hours, or where the authority permits, a lesser period, ending after 7 pm, (evening meal allowance), £8.38.

(b) in the case of an absence overnight from the usual place of residence £79.82 and for such an absence overnight in London, or for the purposes of attendance at an annual conference (including or not including an annual meeting) of the Local Government Association or such other association of bodies as the Secretaries of State may for the time being approve for the purpose,[1] £91.04.

(2) For the purposes of this paragraph, London means the City of London and the London boroughs of Camden, Greenwich, Hackney, Hammersmith and Fulham, Islington, Kensington and Chelsea, Lambeth, Lewisham, Southwark, Tower Hamlets, Wandsworth and Westminster.

2. Any rate determined under paragraph 1(b) above shall be deemed to cover a continuous period of absence of 24 hours.

3. The rates specified in paragraph 1 above shall be reduced by an appropriate amount in respect of any meal provided free of charge by an authority or body in respect of the meal or the period to which the allowance relates.

---

[1] The annual conferences of the following Associations are approved for these purposes: the Association of British Market Authorities, the British Resorts Association, the Council of Local Education Authorities and the National Association of Local Councils.

4.—(1) Where main meals (i.e breakfast, lunch or dinner) are taken on trains during a period for which there is an entitlement to a day subsistence allowance, the reasonable cost of the meals (including VAT), may be reimbursed in full, within the limits specified below. In such circumstances, reimbursement for the reasonable cost of a meal would replace the entitlement to the day subsistence allowance for the appropriate meal period.

(2) The limitations on reimbursement are:

(a) for breakfast, an absence of more than 4 hours, or where the authority permits, a lesser period, before 11am;

(b) for lunch, an absence of more than 4 hours, or where the authority permits, a lesser period, including the period between 12 noon and 2pm;

(c) for dinner, an absence of more than 4 hours, or where the authority permits, a lesser period, ending after 7pm.

EXECUTIVE ARRANGEMENTS – REGULATIONS, CIRCULARS AND GUIDANCE

Regulations

Local Authorities (Proposals for Alternative Arrangements) (England) Regulations 2000 (S.I. No. 2850)

Local Authorities (Arrangements for the Discharge of Functions) (England) Regulations 2000 (S.I. 2000 No. 2851)

Local Authorities (Referendums) (Petitions and Directions) (England) Regulations 2000 (S.I. 2000 No. 2852)

Local Authorities (Functions and Responsibilities) (England) Regulations 2000 (S.I. 2000 No. 2853)

Local Authorities (Changing Executive Arrangements and Alternative Arrangements) (England) Regulations 2001 (S.I. 2001 No. 1003)

The respective Welsh regulations are:

The Local Authorities (Proposals for Alternative Arrangements) (Wales) Regulations 2001 (S.I. 2001 No. 2293 (W.181)); the Local Authorities (Referendums) (Petitions and Directions) (Wales) Regulations 2001 (S.I. 2001 No. 2292 (W.180)); the Local Authorities (Executive Arrangements) (Functions and Responsibilities) (Wales) Regulations 2001 (S.I. 2001 No. 2291 (W.179)); the Local Authorities (Executive Arrangements) (Discharge of Functions) (Wales) Regulations 2001 (S.I. 2001 No. 2287 (W.175)); and the Local Authorities (Alternative Arrangements) (Wales) Regulations 2001 (S.I. 2001 No. 2284 (W.173)).

Circulars and Guidance

Department of Transport, Local Government and the Regions — *New Council Constitutions: Local Government Act 2000; Guidance to English Local Authorities*

National Assembly for Wales — *Local Government Act 2000 Part II: Guidance for County and County Borough Councils on Executive Arrangements*

STANDING ORDERS

This Appendix contains—

(1) The Local Authorities (Standing Orders) Regulations 1993

(2) The Local Authorities (Standing Orders) (England) Regulations 2001

(1) THE LOCAL AUTHORITIES (STANDING ORDERS) REGULATIONS 1993

S.I. 1993 No. 202 (as amended by the Local Authorities (Standing Orders) (England) Regulations 2001 – S.I. 2001 No. 3384)

Made	*4th February 1993*
Laid before Parliament	*12th February 1993*
Coming into force	*1st April 1993*

The Secretary of State for the Environment as respects England and the Secretary of State for Wales as respects Wales, in exercise of the powers conferred on them by sections 8, 20 and 190 of the Local Government and Housing Act 1989, and of all other powers enabling them in that behalf, hereby make the following Regulations:

PART I

PRELIMINARY

Citation, commencement and interpretation

1.—(1) These Regulations may be cited as the Local Authorities (Standing Orders) Regulations 1993 and shall come into force on 1st April 1993.

(2) In these Regulations—

"the Act" means the Local Government and Housing Act 1989;

"chief officer", in relation to a relevant authority, means—

- (a) the head of their paid service, designated under section 4(1) of the Act;
- (b) their monitoring officer;
- (c) a statutory chief officer mentioned in paragraph (a), (c) or (d) of section 2(6) of the Act; or
- (d) a non-statutory chief officer (within the meaning of section 2(7) of the Act);

and any reference to an appointment or purported appointment of a chief officer includes a reference to the engagement or purported engagement of such an officer under a contract of employment;

"the Common Council" means the Common Council of the City of London in its capacity as a local authority, police authority or port health authority;

"monitoring officer" means the officer designated under section 5(1) of the Act;

"relevant authority" means a county or district council, the council of a London borough, the Common Council and the Council of the Isles of Scilly; and

"relevant joint committee", in relation to an authority, means a joint committee on which the authority are represented.

PART II
STANDING ORDERS RELATING TO CHIEF OFFICERS

Standing orders

2. No later than the first ordinary meeting of the authority

falling after the day on which these Regulations come into force, a relevant authority shall, in respect of the appointment of its chief officers—

  (a) make standing orders incorporating—

    (i)   the provisions set out in Part I of Schedule 1 of these Regulations; or

    (ii) provisions to the like effect; or

    (iii) provisions incorporating the effect of those provisions modified as provided in Part II of that Schedule; and

  (b) modify any existing standing orders of theirs in so far as is necessary to conform with those provisions;

and shall not thereafter vary standing orders so made or modified other than by way of incorporating provision having effect as described in Part II of that Schedule.

  (3) A relevant authority shall pay the remuneration of a relevant designated independent person, and any costs incurred by him in or in conection with the discharge of his functions under this regulation.

  3. *[Revoked.]*

PART III

STANDING ORDERS RELATING TO MEETINGS AND PROCEEDINGS

Meetings and proceedings

  4.—(1) No later than the first ordinary meeting of the authority falling after the day on which these Regulations come into force, a county or district council, the council of a London borough and the Council of the Isles of Scilly shall, in respect of the matters mentioned in paragraph (2)—

  (a) make standing orders incorporating the provisions

set out in Schedule 2 to these Regulations, or provisions to the like effect; and

(b) modify any existing standing orders in so far as is necessary to conform with those provisions.

(2) The matters referred to in paragraph (1) are—

(a) the recording of votes of the authority or any of their committees or sub-committees, or of any relevant joint committee, or sub-committee of such a committee; and

(b) the signing of minutes of the authority.

SCHEDULE 1 Regulation 2
Standing Orders Relating to Chief Officers

PART I
PRESCRIBED STANDING ORDERS

Appointments

1. Where the authority propose to appoint a chief officer within the meaning of the Local Authrities (Standing Orders) (England) Regulations 1993), and it is not proposed that the appointment be made exclusively from among their existing officers, they shall—

(a) draw up a statement specifying—

    (i) the duties of the officer concerned, and

    (ii) any qualifications or qualities to be sought in the person to be appointed;

(b) make arrangements for the post to be advertised in such a way as is likely to bring it to the attention of persons who are qualified to apply for it; and

(c) make arrangements for a copy of the statement mentioned in paragraph (a) to be sent to any person on request.

2.—(1) Where a post has been advertised as provided in standing order 1(b), the authority shall—

(a) interview all qualified applicants for the post, or

(b) select a short list of such qualified applicants and interview those included on the short list.

(2) Where no qualified person has applied, the authority shall make further arrangements for advertisement in accordance with standing order 1(b).

PART II
AUTHORISED VARIATIONS

1. The standing orders may provide that—

(a) the steps taken under standing order 1 or 2 above may be taken by a committee, sub-committee or chief officer of the authority;

(b) any chief officer may be appointed by a committee or sub-committee of the authority, or a relevant joint committee.

2. The standing orders may provide that where the duties of a chief officer include the discharge of functions of two or more local authorities in pursuance of section 101(5) of the Local Government Act 1972—

(a) the steps taken under standing order 1 or 2 above may be taken by a joint committee of those authorities, a sub-committee of that committee or a chief officer of any of the authorities concerned; and

(b) any chief officer may be appointed by such a joint committee, a sub-committee of that committee or a committee or sub-committee of any of those authorities.

3. There may be excluded from the application of standing orders 1 to 3—

(a) any appointment of a non-statutory chief officer (within the meaning of section 2(7)(a) or (b) of the Act), and

(b) any appointment in pursuance of section 9 (assistants for political groups) of the Act, and

(c) any appointment in pursuance of regulations made under paragraph 6 of Schedule 1 to the Local Government Act 2000 (mayor's assistant).

4. *[Revoked.]*

SCHEDULE 2   Regulation 4

Standing Orders Relating to Meetings and Proceedings

Recording of votes

1.—(1) Where immediately after a vote is taken at a meeting of a relevant body any member of that body so requires, there shall be recorded in the minutes of the proceedings of that meeting whether that person cast his vote for the question or against the question or whether he abstained from voting.

(2) In this paragraph "relevant body" means the authority, a committee or sub-committee of the authority or a relevant joint committee or sub-committee of such a committee.

Signing minutes — extraordinary meetings

2. Where in relation to any meeting of the authority the next such meeting is a meeting called under paragraph 3 (extraordinary meetings) of Schedule 12 to the Local Government Act 1972, the next following meeting of the authority (being a meeting called otherwise than under that paragraph) shall be treated as a suitable meeting for the purposes of paragraph 41(1) and (2) (signing of minutes) of that Schedule.

(2) THE LOCAL AUTHORITIES (STANDING ORDERS) (ENGLAND) REGULATIONS 2001
S.I. 2001 No. 3384

Made	*10th October 2001*
Laid before Parliament	*17th October 2001*
Coming into force	*7th November 2001*

The Secretary of State for Transport, Local Government and the Regions, in exercise of the powers conferred on him by sections 8, 20 and 190 of the Local Government and Housing Act 1989 and sections 19 and 26 of the Local Government Act 1992, and of all other powers enabling him in that behalf, hereby makes the following Regulations:

Citation, commencement and extent

1.—(1)   These Regulations may be cited as the Local Authorities (Standing Orders) (England) Regulations 2001 and shall come into force on 7th November 2001.

(2) These Regulations extend to England only and, accordingly, references in these Regulations to an authority are references to an authority in England.

Interpretation

2.   In these Regulations—

"the 1989 Act" means the Local Government and Housing Act 1989;

"the 2000 Act" means the Local Government Act 2000;

"the 1993 Regulations" means the Local Authorities (Standing Orders) Regulations 1993;

"alternative arrangements" has the same meaning as in Part II of the 2000 Act (arrangements with respect to executives etc.);

"chief finance officer" means the officer having responsibility, for the purposes of—

(a) section 151 of the Local Government Act 1972 (financial administration); or

(b) section 6 of the 1989 Act (officer responsible for financial administration of certain authorities), for the administration of the local authority's financial affairs;

"council manager" has the same meaning as in section 11(4)(b) of the 2000 Act;

"disciplinary action" in relation to a member of staff of a local authority means any action occasioned by alleged misconduct which, if proved, would, according to the usual practice of the authority, be recorded on the member of staff's personal file, and includes any proposal for dismissal of a member of staff for any reason other than redundancy, permanent ill-health or infirmity of mind or body, but does not include failure to renew a contract of employment for a fixed term unless the authority has undertaken to renew such a contract;

"elected mayor", "executive", "executive arrangements" and "executive leader" have the same meaning as in Part II of the 2000 Act;

"head of the authority's paid service" means the officer designated under section 4(1) of the 1989 Act (designation and reports of head of (paid service);

"local authority" means—

(a) a relevant authority;

(b) the Common Council of the City of London in its capacity as a local authority, police authority or port health authority; or

(c) the Council of the Isles of Scilly;

"member of staff" means a person appointed to or holding a paid office or employment; under a relevant authority;

"monitoring officer" means the officer designated under section 5(1) of the 1989 Act (designation and reports of monitoring officer);

"plan or strategy" means—

(a) a plan or strategy of a description specified in column (1) of the table in Schedule 3 to the Local Authorities (Functions and Responsibilities) (England) Regulations 2000 (functions not to be the sole responsibility of an authority's executive), as amended from time to time;

(b) a plan or strategy for the control of a relevant authority's borrowing or capital expenditure; or

(c) any other plan or strategy whose adoption or approval is, by virtue of regulation 5(1) of the Local Authorities (Functions and Responsibilities) (England) Regulations 2000 (discharge of executive functions by authorities) as amended from time to time, a matter for determination by a relevant authority;

"relevant authority" means a county council, a district council or a London borough council; and

"working day" means any day which is not a Saturday, a Sunday, Christmas Eve, Christmas Day, Maundy Thursday, Good Friday, a bank holiday in England or a day appointed for public thanksgiving or mourning; and

"bank holiday" means a day to be observed as such under section 1 of and Schedule 1 to the Banking and Financial Dealings Act 1971.

Executive arrangements – standing orders relating to staff, proceedings and business

3.—(1) Subject to paragraphs (3) and (4) of regulation 10, on or before the date on which a relevant authority starts to operate executive arrangements under Part II of the 2000 Act—

- (a) if its executive is to take the form specified in section 11(2) of the 2000 Act (mayor and cabinet executive), it must—
  - (i) incorporate in standing orders relating to its staff the provisions set out in Part I of Schedule 1 or provisions to the like effect; and
  - (ii) incorporate in standing orders for regulating its proceedings and business the provisions set out in Part I of Schedule 2 or provisions to the like effect;
- (b) if its executive is to take the form specified in section 11(3) of the 2000 Act (leader and cabinet executive), it must—
  - (i) incorporate in standing orders relating to its staff the provisions set out in Part II of Schedule 1 or provisions to the like effect; and
  - (ii) incorporate in standing orders for regulating its proceedings and business the provisions set out in Part II of Schedule 2 or provisions to the like effect;
- (c) if its executive is to take the form specified in section 11(4) of the 2000 Act (mayor and council manager executive), it must—
  - (i) incorporate in standing orders relating to its staff the provisions set out in Part III of Schedule 1 or provisions to the like effect; and

    (ii) incorporate in standing orders for regulating its proceedings and business the provisions set out in Part I of Schedule 2 or provisions to the like effect; and

  (d) it must modify any of its existing standing orders in so far as is necessary to conform with the provisions referred to in sub-paragraphs (a), (b) and (c).

  (2) A relevant authority which has incorporated provisions in standing orders pursuant to paragraph (1) must, where it proposes to change its executive arrangements so that its executive will take a different form, make variations to its standing orders to the extent necessary to conform with the provisions referred to in sub-paragraph (a), (b), (c) or (d) of paragraph (1), as the case may be, on or before the date on which it starts to operate those changed executive arrangements.

Alternative arrangements – standing orders relating to staff

  4. Subject to paragraphs (3) and (4) of regulation 10, on or before the date on which a relevant authority starts to operate alternative arrangements under Part II of the 2000 Act it must—

  (a) incorporate in standing orders relating to its staff the provisions set out in Part IV of Schedule 1 or provisions to the like effect; and

  (b) modify any of its existing standing orders in so far as is necessary to conform with the provisions referred to in sub-paragraph (a).

Standing orders relating to staff

  5. Where a relevant authority has standing orders incorporating the provisions in paragraph 4(1) of Part I, paragraph 4(1) of Part II or paragraph 4 of Part IV of Schedule

1 (or provisions to the like effect), the power to approve the appointment or dismissal of the head of the authority's paid service shall be exercised by the authority itself and accordingly section 101 of the Local Government Act 1972 (arrangements for discharge of functions by local authorities) shall not apply to the exercise of that power.

Standing orders in respect of disciplinary action

6.   No later than the first ordinary meeting of the local authority falling after the day on which these Regulations come into force, a local authority must, in respect of disciplinary action against the head of the authority's paid service, its monitoring officer and its chief finance officer—

(a) incorporate in standing orders the provisions set out in Schedule 3 or provisions to the like effect; and

(b) modify any of its existing standing orders in so far as is necessary to conform with those provisions.

Investigation of alleged misconduct

7.—(1)   Subject to paragraph (5), where, after a local authority has incorporated provisions in standing orders pursuant to regulation 6, it appears to the local authority that an allegation of misconduct by—

(a) the head of the authority's paid service;

(b) its monitoring officer; or

(c) its chief finance officer,

as the case may be, ("the relevant officer"), requires to be investigated, the authority must appoint a person ("the designated independent person") for the purposes of the standing order which incorporates the provisions in Schedule 3 (or provisions to the like effect).

(2) The designated independent person must be such

person as may be agreed between the authority and the relevant officer or, in default of such agreement, nominated by the Secretary of State.

(3) The designated independent person—

(a) may direct—

    (i) that the authority terminate any suspension of the relevant officer;

    (ii) that any such suspension must continue after the expiry of the period referred to in paragraph 3 of Schedule 3 (or in provisions to the like effect);

    (iii) that the terms on which any such suspension has taken place must be varied in accordance with the direction; or

    (iv) that no steps (whether by the authority or any committee, sub-committee or officer acting on behalf of the authority) towards disciplinary action or further disciplinary action against the relevant officer, other than steps taken in the presence, or with the agreement, of the designated independent person, are to be taken before a report is made under sub-paragraph (d);

(b) may inspect any documents relating to the conduct of the relevant officer which are in the possession of the authority, or which the authority has power to authorise him to inspect;

(c) may require any member of staff of the authority to answer questions concerning the conduct of the relevant officer;

(d) must make a report to the authority—

    (i) stating his opinion as to whether (and, if so, the extent to which) the evidence he has obtained supports any allegation of misconduct against the relevant officer; and

(ii) recommending any disciplinary action which appears to him to be appropriate for the authority to take against the relevant officer; and

(e) must no later than the time at which he makes his report under sub-paragraph (d), send a copy of the report to the relevant officer.

(4) A local authority must pay reasonable remuneration to a designated independent person appointed by the authority and any costs incurred by him in, or in connection with, the discharge of his functions under this regulation.

(5) This regulation shall not apply in relation to the head of the authority's paid service if he is also the council manager of the authority.

Amendments to the 1993 Regulations

8.—(1) In Schedule 1 to the 1993 Regulations (standing orders relating to chief officers), in so far as it extends to England—

(a) in paragraph 1 of Part I (appointments), after "chief officer", there shall be inserted "(within the meaning of the Local Authorities (Standing Orders) Regulations 1993)"; and

(b) in paragraph 3 of Part II (authorised variations), at the end of paragraph (b) there shall be added—

", and

(c) any appointment in pursuance of regulations made under paragraph 6 of Schedule 1 to the Local Government Act 2000 (mayor's assistant)."

(2) Subject to paragraph (3), the following provisions of

the 1993 Regulations shall be revoked in so far as those provisions extend to England—

(a) in regulation 1(2) (interpretation), the words "disciplinary action" and the definition of that term;

(b) in regulation 2 (standing orders), the words "and disciplinary action against the head of its paid service";

(c) regulation 3 (investigation of alleged misconduct); and

(d) paragraph 3 (appointments) and paragraph 4 (disciplinary action) of Part I of Schedule 1.

(3) Paragraph (2) shall not apply in relation to a National Park authority in England.

Amendments to the Local Government Changes for England Regulations 1994

9. In regulation 11 of the Local Government Changes for England Regulations 1994 (functions and powers of the shadow authority)—

(a) in paragraph (7), for "The shadow authority", there shall be substituted "Subject to paragraph (9), the shadow authority";

(b) at the end of paragraph (7), there shall be added—

"; and

(k) the Local Authorities (Standing Orders) (England) Regulations 2001"; and

(c) after paragraph (8), there shall be added—

"(9) Sub-paragraph (k) of paragraph (7) shall only apply in relation to a shadow authority which will become a county council in England, a district council or a London borough council.".

Transitional and consequential provisions

10.—(1) Subject to paragraph (2), where a local authority made standing orders incorporating the provisions set out in paragraph 4 of Part I of Schedule 1 to the 1993 Regulations (or provisions to the like effect), until the authority incorporates provisions in standing orders in accordance with regulation 6—

(a) those standing orders shall continue in force; and

(b) regulation 7 shall apply in relation to them in respect of the head of the authority's paid service, as it does in relation to standing orders which incorporate provisions in accordance with regulation 6.

(2) Anything which, before the date on which the local authority incorporated provisions in standing orders in accordance with regulation 6, was being done by, to or in relation to an officer in accordance with—

(a) regulation 3 of the 1993 Regulations;

(b) the provisions set out in paragraph 4 of Part I of Schedule 1 to the 1993 Regulations (or provisions to the like effect) incorporated in the local authority's standing orders; or

(c) regulation 7 as applied by paragraph (1)(b), may be continued after that date by, to or in relation to him in accordance with the provisions referred to in sub-paragraphs (a), (b) or (c), as the case may be.

(3) Where a relevant authority—

(a) sent a copy of proposals to the Secretary of State, before the date on which these Regulations come into force, under—

(i) section 25 of the 2000 Act (proposals); or

(ii) regulations made under section 31 of the 2000

Act (alternative arrangements in case of certain local authorities); and

(b) had not started to operate executive arrangements or alternative arrangements before that date, if the authority considers that it would be impracticable to comply with the requirements of regulation 3 or, as the case may be, regulation 4 on or before the date on which it starts to operate executive arrangements or alternative arrangements, it shall comply with those requirements as soon as reasonably practicable after it has started to operate those arrangements.

(4) Where a relevant authority started to operate executive arrangements or alternative arrangements before the date on which these Regulations come into force, it shall comply with the requirements of regulation 3 or, as the case may be, regulation 4 as soon as reasonably practicable after that date.

SCHEDULE 1
Provisions to be Incorporated in Standing Orders relating to Staff

PART I
AUTHORITY WITH MAYOR AND CABINET EXECUTIVE

1. In this Part—

"the 1989 Act" means the Local Government and Housing Act 1989;

"the 2000 Act" means the Local Government Act 2000;

"disciplinary action" has the same meaning as in the Local Authorities (Standing Orders) (England) Regulations 2001;

"elected mayor" and "executive" have the same meaning as in Part II of the 2000 Act;

"member of staff" means a person appointed to or holding a paid office or employment under the authority;

and

"proper officer" means an officer appointed by the authority for the purposes of the provisions in this Part.

2. Subject to paragraphs 3 and 7, the function of appointment and dismissal of, and taking disciplinary action against, a member of staff of the authority must be discharged, on behalf of the authority, by the officer designated under section 4(1) of the 1989 Act (designation and reports of head of paid service) as the head of the authority's paid service or by an officer nominated by him.

3. Paragraph 2 shall not apply to the appointment or dismissal of, or disciplinary action against—

(a) the officer designated as the head of the authority's paid service;

(b) a statutory chief officer within the meaning of section 2(6) of the 1989 Act (politically restricted posts);

(c) a non-statutory chief officer within the meaning of section 2(7) of the 1989 Act;

(d) a deputy chief officer within the meaning of section 2(8) of the 1989 Act;

(e) a person appointed in pursuance of section 9 of the 1989 Act (assistants for political groups); or

(f) a person appointed in pursuance of regulations under paragraph 6 of Schedule 1 to the 2000 Act (mayor's assistant).

4.—(1) Where a committee, sub-committee or officer is discharging, on behalf of the authority, the function of the appointment or dismissal of an officer designated as the head of the authority's paid service, the authority must approve that appointment before an offer of appointment is made to him or, as the case may be, must approve that dismissal before notice of dismissal is given to him.

(2) Where a committee or a sub-committee of the authority is discharging, on behalf of the authority, the function of the appointment or dismissal of any officer referred to in sub-paragraphs (a), (b), (c) or d) of paragraph 3, at least one member of the executive must be a member of that committee or sub-committee.

5.—(1) In this paragraph, "appointor" means, in relation to the appointment of a person as an officer of the authority, the authority or, where a committee, sub-committee or officer is discharging the function of appointment on behalf of the authority, that committee, sub-committee or officer, as the case may be.

(2) An offer of an appointment as an officer referred to in sub-paragraph (a), (b), (c) or (d) of paragraph 3 must not be made by the appointor until—

(a) the appointor has notified the proper officer of the name of the person to whom the appointor wishes to make the offer and any other particulars which the appointor considers are relevant to the appointment;

(b) the proper officer has notified every member of the executive of the authority of—

(i) the name of the person to whom the appointor wishes to make the offer;

(ii) any other particulars relevant to the appointment which the appointor has notified to the proper officer; and

(iii) the period within which any objection to the making of the offer is to be made by the elected mayor on behalf of the executive to the proper officer; and

(c) either—

(i) the elected mayor has, within the period specified

in the notice under sub-paragraph (b)(iii), notified the appointor that neither he nor any other member of the executive has any objection to the making of the offer;

(ii) the proper officer has notified the appointor that no objection was received by him within that period from the elected mayor; or

(iii) the appointor is satisfied that any objection received from the elected mayor within that period is not material or is not well-founded.

6.—(1) In this paragraph, "dismissor" means, in relation to the dismissal of an officer of the authority, the authority or, where a committee, sub-committee or another officer is discharging the function of dismissal on behalf of the authority, that committee, sub-committee or other officer, as the case may be.

(2) Notice of the dismissal of an officer referred to in sub-paragraph (a), (b), (c) or (d) of paragraph 3 must not be given by the dismissor until—

(a) the dismissor has notified the proper officer of the name of the person who the dismissor wishes to dismiss and any other particulars which the dismissor considers are relevant to the dismissal;

(b) the proper officer has notified every member of the executive of the authority of—

(i) the name of the person who the dismissor wishes to dismiss;

(ii) any other particulars relevant to the dismissal which the dismissor has notified to the proper officer; and

(iii) the period within which any objection to the

dismissal is to be made by the elected mayor on behalf of the executive to the proper officer; and

(c) either—

   (i) the elected mayor has, within the period specified in the notice under sub-paragraph (b)(iii), notified the dismissor that neither he nor any other member of the executive has any objection to the dismissal;

   (ii) the proper officer has notified the dismissor that no objection was received by him within that period from the elected mayor; or

   (iii) the dismissor is satisfied that any objection received from the elected mayor within that period is not material or is not well-founded.

7. Nothing in paragraph 2 shall prevent a person from serving as a member of any committee or sub-committee established by the authority to consider an appeal by—

(a) another person against any decision relating to the appointment of that other person as a member of staff of the authority; or

(b) a member of staff of the authority against any decision relating to the dismissal of, or taking disciplinary action against, that member of staff.

PART II
AUTHORITY WITH LEADER AND CABINET EXECUTIVE

1. In this Part—

"the 1989 Act" means the Local Government and Housing Act 1989;

"the 2000 Act" means the Local Government Act 2000;

"disciplinary action" has the same meaning as in the Local Authorities (Standing Orders) (England) Regulations 2001;

"executive" and "executive leader" have the same meaning as in Part II of the 2000 Act;

"member of staff" means a person appointed to or holding a paid office or employment under the authority; and

"proper officer" means an officer appointed by the authority for the purposes of the provisions in this Part.

2.   Subject to paragraphs 3 and 7, the function of appointment and dismissal of, and taking disciplinary action against, a member of staff of the authority must be discharged, on behalf of the authority, by the officer designated under section 4(1) of the 1989 Act (designation and reports of head of paid service) as the head of the authority's paid ervice or by an officer nominated by him.

3.   Paragraph 2 shall not apply to the appointment or dismissal of, or disciplinary action against—

(a) the officer designated as the head of the authority's paid service;

(b) a statutory chief officer within the meaning of section 2(6) of the 1989 Act (politically restricted posts);

(c) a non-statutory chief officer within the meaning of section 2(7) of the 1989 Act;

(d) a deputy chief officer within the meaning of section 2(8) of the 1989 Act; or

(e) a person appointed in pursuance of section 9 of the 1989 Act (assistants for political groups).

4.—(1) Where a committee, sub-committee or officer is discharging, on behalf of the authority, the function of the appointment or dismissal of an officer designated as the head of the authority's paid service, the authority must approve that appointment before an offer of appointment is made to him or, as the case may be, must approve that dismissal before notice of dismissal is given to him.

(2) Where a committee or a sub-committee of the authority is discharging, on behalf of the authority, the function of the appointment or dismissal of any officer referred to in sub-paragraph (a), (b), (c) or (d) of paragraph 3, at least one member of the executive must be a member of that committee or sub-committee.

5.—(1) In this paragraph, "appointor" means, in relation to the appointment of a person as an officer of the authority, the authority or, where a committee, sub-committee or officer is discharging the function of appointment on behalf of the authority, that committee, sub-committee or officer, as the case may be.

(2) An offer of an appointment as an officer referred to in sub-paragraph (a), (b), (c) or (d) of paragraph 3 must not be made by the appointor until—

(a) the appointor has notified the proper officer of the name of the person to whom the appointor wishes to make the offer and any other particulars which the appointor considers are relevant to the appointment;

(b) the proper officer has notified every member of the executive of the authority of—

   (i) the name of the person to whom the appointor wishes to make the offer;

   (ii) any other particulars relevant to the appointment which the appointor has notified to the proper officer; and

   (iii) the period within which any objection to the making of the offer is to be made by the executive leader on behalf of the executive to the proper officer; and

(c) either—

    (i) the executive leader has, within the period specified in the notice under sub-paragraph (b)(iii), notified the appointor that neither he nor any other member of the executive has any objection to the making of the offer;

    (ii) the proper officer has notified the appointor that no objection was received by him within that period from the executive leader; or

    (iii) the appointor is satisfied that any objection received from the executive leader within that period is not material or is not well-founded.

6.—(1) In this paragraph, "dismissor" means, in relation to the dismissal of an officer of the authority, the authority or, where a committee, sub-committee or another officer is discharging the function of dismissal on behalf of the authority, that committee, sub-committee or other officer, as the case may be.

(2) Notice of the dismissal of an officer referred to in sub-paragraph (a), (b), (c) or (d) of paragraph 3 must not be given by the dismissor until—

(a) the dismissor has notified the proper officer of the name of the person who the dismissor wishes to dismiss and any other particulars which the dismissor considers are relevant to the dismissal;

(b) the proper officer has notified every member of the executive of the authority of—

    (i) the name of the person who the dismissor wishes to dismiss;

    (ii) any other particulars relevant to the dismissal which the dismissor has notified to the proper officer; and

(iii) the period within which any objection to the dismissal is to be made by the executive leader on behalf of the executive to the proper officer; and

(c) either—

(i) the executive leader has, within the period specified in the notice under sub-paragraph (b)(iii), notified the dismissor that neither he nor any other member of the executive has any objection to the dismissal;

(ii) the proper officer has notified the dismissor that no objection was received by him within that period from the executive leader; or

(iii) the dismissor is satisfied that any objection received from the executive leader within that period is not material or is not well-founded.

7.   Nothing in paragraph 2 shall prevent a person from serving as a member of any committee or sub-committee established by the authority to consider an appeal by—

(a) another person against any decision relating to the appointment of that other person as a member of staff of the authority; or

(b) a member of staff of the authority against any decision relating to the dismissal of, or taking disciplinary action against, that member of staff.

PART III
AUTHORITY WITH MAYOR AND COUNCIL MANAGER EXECUTIVE

1.   In this Part—

"the 2000 Act" means the Local Government Act 2000;

"council manager" has the same meaning as in section 11(4)(b) of the 2000 Act;

"disciplinary action" has the same meaning as in the Local Authorities (Standing Orders) (England) Regulations 2001; and

"member of staff" means a person appointed to or holding a paid office or employment under the authority.

2. Subject to paragraphs 3 and 4, the function of appointment and dismissal of, and taking disciplinary action against, a member of staff of the authority must be discharged, on behalf of the authority, by the council manager or by an officer nominated by him.

3. Paragraph 2 shall not apply to the appointment or dismissal of, or disciplinary action against—

(a) the council manager;

(b) a person appointed in pursuance of section 9 of the Local Government and Housing 1989 Act (assistants for political groups); or

(c) a person appointed in pursuance of regulations under paragraph 6 of Schedule 1 to the 2000 Act (mayor's assistant).

4. Nothing in paragraph 2 shall prevent a person from serving as a member of any committee or sub-committee established by the authority to consider an appeal—

(a) by another person against any decision relating to the appointment of that other person as a member of staff of the authority; or

(b) a member of staff of the authority against any decision relating to the dismissal of, or taking disciplinary action against, that member of staff.

PART IV
AUTHORITY OPERATING ALTERNATIVE ARRANGEMENTS

1. In this Part—

"the 1989 Act" means the Local Government and Housing Act 1989;

"disciplinary action" has the same meaning as in the Local Authorities (Standing Orders) (England) Regulations 2001; and

"member of staff" means a person appointed to or holding a paid office or employment under the authority.

2. Subject to paragraphs 3 and 5, the function of appointment and dismissal of, and taking disciplinary action against, a member of staff of the authority must be discharged, on behalf of the authority, by the officer designated under section 4(1) of the 1989 Act (designation and reports of head of paid service) as the head of the authority's paid service or by an officer nominated by him.

3. Paragraph 2 shall not apply to the appointment or dismissal of, or disciplinary action against—

(a) the officer designated as the head of the authority's paid service;

(b) a statutory chief officer within the meaning of section 2(6) of the 1989 Act (politically restricted posts);

(c) a non-statutory chief officer within the meaning of section 2(7) of the 1989 Act;

(d) a deputy chief officer within the meaning of section 2(8) of the 1989 Act; or

(e) a person appointed in pursuance of section 9 of the 1989 Act (assistants for political groups).

4. Where a committee, sub-committee or officer is

discharging, on behalf of the authority, the function of the appointment or dismissal of an officer designated as the head of the authority's paid service, the authority must approve that appointment before an offer of appointment is made to him or, as the case may be, must approve that dismissal before notice of dismissal is given to him.

5.   Nothing in paragraph 2 shall prevent a person from serving as a member of any committee or sub-committee established by the authority to consider an appeal by—

(a) another person against any decision relating to the appointment of that other person as a member of staff of the authority; or

(b) a member of staff of the authority against any decision relating to the dismissal of, or taking disciplinary action against, that member of staff.

SCHEDULE 2
Provisions to be Incorporated in Standing Orders Regulating Proceedings and Business

PART I
AUTHORITY WITH MAYOR AND CABINET EXECUTIVE OR MAYOR AND
COUNCIL MANAGER EXECUTIVE

1.   In this Part—

"elected mayor" and "executive" have the same meaning as in Part II of the Local Government Act 2000; and

"plan or strategy" and "working day" have the same meaning as in the Local Authorities (Standing Orders) (England) Regulations 2001.

2.   Where the executive of the authority has submitted a draft plan or strategy to the authority for its consideration and, following consideration of that draft plan or strategy, the authority has any objections to it, the authority must take the action set out in paragraph 3.

3. Before the authority—

(a) amends the draft plan or strategy;

(b) approves, for the purpose of its submission to the Secretary of State or any Minister of the Crown for his approval, any plan or strategy (whether or not in the form of a draft) of which any part is required to be so submitted; or

(c) adopts (with or without modification) the plan or strategy, it must inform the elected mayor of any objections which it has to the draft plan or strategy and must give to him instructions requiring the executive to reconsider, in the light of those objections, the draft plan or strategy submitted to it.

4. Where the authority gives instructions in accordance with paragraph 3, it must specify a period of at least five working days beginning on the day after the date on which the elected mayor receives the instructions on behalf of the executive within which the elected mayor may—

(a) submit a revision of the draft plan or strategy as amended by the executive (the "revised draft plan or strategy"), with the executive's reasons for any amendments made to the draft plan or strategy, to the authority for the authority's consideration; or

(b) inform the authority of any disagreement that the executive has with any of the authority's objections and the executive's reasons for any such disagreement.

5. Subject to paragraph 6, when the period specified by the authority, referred to in paragraph 4, has expired, the authority must, when—

(a) amending the draft plan or strategy or, if there is one, the revised draft plan or strategy;

(b) approving, for the purpose of its submission to the

Secretary of State or any Minister of the Crown for his approval, any plan or strategy (whether or not in the form of a draft or revised draft) of which any part is required to be so submitted; or

(c) adopting (with or without modifications) the plan or strategy, take into account any amendments made to the draft plan or strategy that are included in any revised draft plan or strategy, the executive's reasons for those amendments, any disagreement that the executive has with any of the authority's objections and the executive's reasons for that disagreement, which the elected mayor submitted to the authority, or informed the authority of, within the period specified.

6. Where the authority proposes to—

(a) amend the draft plan or strategy or, as the case may be, the revised draft plan or strategy;

(b) approve, for the purpose of its submission to the Secretary of State or any Minister of the Crown for his approval, any plan or strategy (whether or not in the form of a draft) of which any part is required to be so submitted; or

(c) adopt with modifications the plan or strategy, and that plan or strategy (whether or not in the form of a draft), with any proposed amendments or modifications, is not in accordance with the draft plan or strategy or, as the case may be, the revised draft plan or strategy, the question whether to amend, to approve or to adopt the plan or strategy must be decided in accordance with paragraph 7.

7. The question referred to in paragraph 6 must be decided by a two thirds majority of the members of the authority present and voting on the question at a meeting of the authority.

8.   Subject to paragraph 14, where, before 8th February in any financial year, the authority's executive submits to the authority for its consideration in relation to the following financial year—

  (a) estimates of the amounts to be aggregated in making a calculation (whether originally or by way of substitute) in accordance with any of sections 32 to 37 or 43 to 49 of the Local Government Finance Act 1992 (calculation of budget requirements etc.);

  (b) estimates of other amounts to be used for the purposes of such a calculation;

  (c) estimates of such a calculation; or

  (d) amounts required to be stated in a precept under Chapter IV of Part I of the Local Government Finance Act 1992 (precepts), and following consideration of those estimates or amounts the authority has any objections to them, it must take the action set out in paragraph 9.

9.   Before the authority makes a calculation (whether originally or by way of substitute) in accordance with any of the sections referred to in paragraph 8(a), or issues a precept under Chapter IV of Part I of the Local Government Finance Act 1992, it must inform the elected mayor of any objections which it has to the executive's estimates or amounts and must give to him instructions requiring the executive to reconsider, in the light of those objections, those estimates and amounts in accordance with the authority's requirements.

10. Where the authority gives instructions in accordance with paragraph 9, it must specify a period of at least five working days beginning on the day after the date on which the elected mayor receives the instructions on behalf of the executive within which the elected mayor may—

  (a) submit a revision of the estimates or amounts as

amended by the executive ("revised estimates or amounts"), which have been reconsidered in accordance with the authority's requirements, with the executive's reasons for any amendments made to the estimates or amounts, to the authority for the authority's consideration; or

(b) inform the authority of any disagreement that the executive has with any of the authority's objections and the executive's reasons for any such disagreement.

11. Subject to paragraph 12, when the period specified by the authority, referred to in paragraph 10, has expired, the authority must, when making calculations (whether originally or by way of substitute) in accordance with the sections referred to in paragraph 8(a), or when issuing a precept under Chapter IV of Part I of the Local Government Finance Act 1992, take into account—

(a) any amendments to the estimates or amounts that are included in any revised estimates or amounts;

(b) the executive's reasons for those amendments;

(c) any disagreement that the executive has with any of the authority's objections; and

(d) the executive's reasons for that disagreement, which the elected mayor submitted to the authority, or informed the authority of, within the period specified.

12. Where the authority, for the purposes of making the calculations or issuing the precept, proposes to use estimates or amounts ("the different estimates or amounts") which are not in accordance with the executive's estimates or amounts or, as the case may be, the executive's revised estimates or amounts, the question whether to use the different estimates or amounts must be decided in accordance with paragraph 13.

13. The question referred to in paragraph 12 must be decided by a two thirds majority of the members of the authority present and voting on the question at a meeting of the authority.

14. Paragraphs 8 to 13 shall not apply in relation to—

(a) calculations or substitute calculations which an authority is required to make in accordance with section 52I, 52J, 52T or 52U of the Local Government Finance Act 1992 (limitation of council tax and precepts); and

(b) amounts stated in a precept issued to give effect to calculations or substitute calculations made in accordance with section 52J or 52U of that Act.

PART II
AUTHORITY WITH LEADER AND CABINET EXECUTIVE

1. In this Part—

"executive" and "executive leader" have the same meaning as in Part II of the Local Government Act 2000; and

"plan or strategy" and "working day" have the same meaning as in the Local Authorities (Standing Orders) (England) Regulations 2001.

2. Where the executive of the authority has submitted a draft plan or strategy to the authority for its consideration and, following consideration of that draft plan or strategy, the authority has any objections to it, the authority must take the action set out in paragraph 3.

3. Before the authority—

(a) amends the draft plan or strategy;

(b) approves, for the purpose of its submission to the Secretary of State or any Minister of the Crown for his approval, any plan or strategy (whether or not in the form of a draft) of which any part is required to be so submitted; or

(c) adopts (with or without modification) the plan or strategy, it must inform the executive leader of any objections which it has to the draft plan or strategy and must give to him instructions requiring the executive to reconsider, in the light of those objections, the draft plan or strategy submitted to it.

4. Where the authority gives instructions in accordance with paragraph 3, it must specify a period of at least five working days beginning on the day after the date on which the executive leader receives the instructions on behalf of the executive within which the executive leader may—

(a) submit a revision of the draft plan or strategy as amended by the executive (the "revised draft plan or strategy"), with the executive's reasons for any amendments made to the draft plan or strategy, to the authority for the authority's consideration; or

(b) inform the authority of any disagreement that the executive has with any of the authority's objections and the executive's reasons for any such disagreement.

5. When the period specified by the authority, referred to in paragraph 4, has expired, the authority must, when—

(a) amending the draft plan or strategy or, if there is one, the revised draft plan or strategy;

(b) approving, for the purpose of its submission to the Secretary of State or any Minister of the Crown for his approval, any plan or strategy (whether or not in the form of a draft or revised draft) of which any part is required to be so submitted; or

(c) adopting (with or without modification) the plan or strategy, take into account any amendments made to the draft plan or strategy that are included in any revised draft plan or strategy, the executive's reasons for those amendments, any disagreement that the executive has with any of the authority's objections and the executive's reasons for that disagreement, which the executive leader submitted to the authority, or informed the authority of, within the period specified.

6. Subject to paragraph 10, where, before 8th February in any financial year, the authority's executive submits to the authority for its consideration in relation to the following financial year—

(a) estimates of the amounts to be aggregated in making a calculation (whether originally or by way of substitute) in accordance with any of sections 32 to 37 or 43 to 49, of the Local Government Finance Act 1992;

(b) estimates of other amounts to be used for the purposes of such a calculation;

(c) estimates of such a calculation; or

(d) amounts required to be stated in a precept under Chapter IV of Part I of the Local Government Finance Act 1992, and following consideration of those estimates or amounts the authority has any objections to them, it must take the action set out in paragraph 7.

7. Before the authority makes a calculation (whether originally or by way of substitute) in accordance with any of the sections referred to in paragraph 6(a), or issues a precept under Chapter IV of Part I of the Local Government Finance Act 1992, it must inform the executive leader of any objections which it has to the executive's estimates or amounts and must give to him instructions requiring the executive to reconsider,

in the light of those objections, those estimates and amounts in accordance with the authority's requirements.

8.   Where the authority gives instructions in accordance with paragraph 7, it must specify a period of at least five working days beginning on the day after the date on which the executive leader receives the instructions on behalf of the executive within which the executive leader may—

(a)   submit a revision of the estimates or amounts as amended by the executive ("revised estimates or amounts"), which have been reconsidered in accordance with the authority's requirements, with the executive's reasons for any amendments made to the estimates or amounts, to the authority for the authority's consideration; or

(b)   inform the authority of any disagreement that the executive has with any of the authority's objections and the executive's reasons for any such disagreement.

9.   When the period specified by the authority, referred to in paragraph 8, has expired, the authority must, when making calculations (whether originally or by way of substitute) in accordance with the sections referred to in paragraph 6(a), or issuing a precept under Chapter IV of Part I of the Local Government Finance Act 1992, take into account—

(a)   any amendments to the estimates or amounts that are included in any revised estimates or amounts;

(b)   the executive's reasons for those amendments;

(c)   any disagreement that the executive has with any of the authority's objections; and

(d)   the executive's reasons for that disagreement, which the executive leader submitted to the authority, or informed the authority of, within the period specified.

10. Paragraphs 6 to 9 shall not apply in relation to—

(a) calculations or substitute calculations which an authority is required to make in accordance with section 52I, 52J, 52T or 52U of the Local Government Finance Act 1992; and

(b) amounts stated in a precept issued to give effect to calculations or substitute calculations made in accordance with section 52J or 52U of that Act.

SCHEDULE 3
Provisions to be Incorporated in Standing Orders in Respect of Disciplinary Action

1. In paragraph 2, "chief finance officer", "council manager", "disciplinary action", "head of the authority's paid service" and "monitoring officer", have the same meaning as in regulation 2 of the Local Authorities (Standing Orders) (England) Regulations 2001 and "designated independent person" has the same meaning as in regulation 7 of those Regulations.

2. No disciplinary action in respect of the head of the authority's paid service (unless he is also a council manager of the authority), its monitoring officer or its chief finance officer, except action described in paragraph 3, may be taken by the authority, or by a committee, a sub-committee, a joint committee on which the authority is represented or any other person acting on behalf of the authority, other than in accordance with a recommendation in a report made by a designated independent person under regulation 7 of the Local Authorities (Standing Orders) (England) Regulations 2001 (investigation of alleged misconduct).

3. The action mentioned in paragraph 2 is suspension of the officer for the purpose of investigating the alleged misconduct occasioning the action; and any such suspension must be on full pay and terminate no later than the expiry of two months beginning on the day on which the suspension takes effect.

USEFUL ADDRESSES

Association of Councillors, Crown Court Buildings, Princess Street, Huddersfield HD1 2TT (tel: 01484 221000).

Association of Larger Local Councils, PO Box 191, Macclesfield, Cheshire SK11 0FG (tel: 01260 226323; fax 01260 226329).

Association of London Government, 36 Old Queen Street, London SW1H 9JF (tel: 020 7222 7799; fax: 020 7799 2339).

Audit Commission, 1 Vincent Square, London SW1P 2BR (tel: 020 7396 1315). Website: www.audit-commission.gov.uk

Chartered Institute of Public Finance and Accountancy (CIPFA), 3 Robert Street, London WC2N 6BH (tel: 020 7543 5600). Website: www.cipfa.org.uk

Commission for Local Administration in England, 21 Queen Anne's Gate, London SW1H 9BU (tel: 0207 915 3210; fax: 020 7233 0396). Website: www.open.gov.uk/lgo

Commission for Local Administration in Wales, Derwen House, Court Road, Bridgend CF31 1BN (tel: 01656 661325; fax: 01656 6583217). Website: www.ombudsman-wales.org

Countryside Agency, John Dower House, Crescent Place, Cheltenham, Glos GL50 3RA (tel: 01242 521381; fax: 01242 584270). Website: www.countryside.gov.uk

Department of Transport, Local Government and the Regions, Eland House, Bressenden Place, London SW1E 5DU (tel (general enquiries): 020 7944 3000). Website: www.detr.gov.uk

Electoral Commission, Trevelyan House, Great Peter

Street, London SW1P 2HW (tel: 020 7271 0500; fax: 020 7271 0505; email: electoral.commission@gtnet.gov.uk). Website: www.electoralcommission.gov.uk

Improvement and Development Agency, Layden House, 76-86 Turnmill Street, London EC1M 5LG (tel: 020 7296 6600; fax: 020 7296 9999). Website: www.idea.gov.uk

Local Councils Advisory Service, 3 Trinity Close, 20 Church Street, Henley-on-Thames, Oxon RG9 1SE (tel and fax 01491 412559; email: clayden@lcaservice.freeserve.co.uk).

Local Government Association, Local Government House, Smith Square, London SW1P 3HZ (tel: 020 7664 3000; fax: 020 7664 3030). Website: www.lga.gov.uk

National Assembly for Wales, Cardiff Bay, Cardiff CF99 1NA (tel: 029 2089200 (general information) and 029 20825111). Website: www.wales.gov.uk

National Association of Local Councils, 109 Great Russell Street, London WC1B 3LD (tel: 020 7637 1865; fax: 020 7436 7451. Website: www.nalc.org.uk

National Joint Council for Local Government Services, Layden House, 76-86 Turnmill Street, London EC1M 5LG (tel: 020 7296 660; fax: 020 7296 6666). Website: www.lg-employers.gov.uk

Society of Local Authority Chief Executives (SOLACE), Hope House, 45 Great Peter Street, London SW1P 3LT (tel: 020 7233 0081). Website: www.solace.org.uk

Society of Local Council Clerks, 1 Fisher Lane, Bingham, Nottingham NG13 8BQ. (tel: 0115 923 2200; fax: 01949 836583). Website: www.slcc.co.uk

Standards Board for England, 5th Floor, St. Christopher House, 98-104 Southwark Street, London SE1 0TE (tel: 020 7921 1807). Website: www.standardsboard.co.uk

Wales Association of Community & Town Councils, Unit 5, Betws Business Park, Park Street, Ammanford SA18 2ET (tel: 01269 595400; email: CcbtcWactc@aol.com).

Welsh Local Government Association, 10-11 Raleigh Walk, Atlantic Wharf, Cardiff CF1 3NQ (tel: 029 2046 8600, fax: 029 2046 8601). Website: www.wlga.org

Appendix F

CONSULTATION PROPOSALS ON TRAVEL, SUBSISTENCE AND OTHER ALLOWANCES; WHITE PAPER ON LOCAL GOVERNMENT

Introduction

The government has (1) made proposals for changes to travel, subsistence and other allowances payable to councillors and co-opted members of local authorities in England, and (2) issued a White Paper entitled *Strong Local Leadership; Quality Public Services* (applying only to England).

(1) ALLOWANCES

Summary of proposals

- Each principal authority is to determine its own travel and subsistence allowances for members having regard to recommendations of its own remuneration panel. Travel and subsistence allowances are to be discretionary allowances. Co-opted and appointed members of a principal council's committees are to be paid a new "meetings allowance", to be determined by the local authority having regard to the recommendations its independent remuneration panel.

- Parish councillors are to be able to receive a new "participation allowance" and travel allowance for travel both within and outside the area of their parish.

- Joint authorities and certain other authorities are to be able to pay co-opted members a "meetings allowance", to be determined by the authority. Joint authorities, other authorities and certain other bodies are to be able to determine their own travel and subsistence allowances

[228]

which will be discretionary allowances. Local authorities and certain other bodies are to be able to pay a cycling allowance to members.

- Allowances for attending meetings and conferences paid under section 175 of the Local Government Act 1972 are to be abolished.

- Combined fire authorities and the Broads Authority to be able to establish a scheme of allowances under section 18 of the Local Government and Housing Act 1989.

- The specified list of duties for which a special responsibility allowance may be payable is to be amended to include certain quasi-judicial duties.

Allowances for principal authorities

1. The following regime of travel and subsistence allowances is proposed for all members of principal authorities, including elected members and non-elected co-opted members, appointed members and members of other bodies appointed or nominated by the principal council.

(a) Travel and subsistence allowances are to be discretionary allowances. This will allow local authorities and others to decide for themselves whether they wish to pay these allowances or to set basic allowance, and meeting allowance in the case of non-elected members, at a level which might reasonably be expected to cover a member's travel and subsistence costs.

(b) Travel and subsistence allowances are to be determined locally with no involvement from the Secretary of State. Local authorities may reimburse actual costs incurred, rather than maintaining an allowances structure, and may establish systems of direct invoicing for, particularly, overnight subsistence. It may be that local authorities will adopt a regime with differing basis of payment depending on the nature and amount of the allowance, but which it is able to operate efficiently and cost effectively.

(c) It will be for each principal authority to determine its scheme for travel and subsistence allowances, having regard to a recommendation of its independent remuneration panel.

(d) Provision is to be made to allow principal authorities to pay a cycling allowance if they wish to do so.

(e) Travel and subsistence allowances may only be paid in respect of those duties specified as "approved duties" by the Secretary of State (see Annex A).

(f) Principal authorities are to be required to keep a record of all payments made by way of travel and subsistence allowances where these are paid. This record must specify the recipient and the amount of the allowance received. The record should be available at all reasonable times for inspection by any local government elector for the area, who may make a copy of any part of it.

2.   The following regime of allowances is proposed for co-opted and appointed members of principal councils and non-elected members of other bodies appointed or nominated by a principal council.

(a) Principal authorities may make provision for the payment of a new meeting allowance to their co-opted members and must make provision for such allowances for their appointed members on the authority's overview and scrutiny committee dealing with education.

(b) Principal authorities may make provision for the payment of a meeting allowance to non-elected members which the authority has appointed or nominated to certain other bodies. These bodies will include joint committees, joint boards, and other combined bodies, a school organisation committee, a school exclusion appeals panel and a school admission appeals panel.

(c) Meeting allowances are to be determined locally, following the recommendation of an independent remuneration panel. The local authority must have regard to the recommendations of its panel in respect of meeting allowances.

(d) The meeting allowance will be an annual allowance which may vary from one co-opted member to another depending on the nature of the co-option, or appointment, and the expected time commitment of the co-optee or appointee.

(e) Where a local authority has both co-opted members and appointed members on its overview and scrutiny committee dealing with education, any meeting allowance paid to a co-opted member must not exceed that made available to appointed members. Further where either a co-opted member or an appointed member is appointed chair of the committee on which they are co-opted or appointed, the meeting allowance which they receive must be of an amount no less than the equivalent special responsibility allowances being made available to chairs of equivalent committees of the council.

Allowances for parish councils

3. The following regime of allowances is proposed for parish councillors—

(a) There is to be a new allowance for parish councillors to be known as a "participation allowance".

(b) A participation allowance will be an annual allowance which a parish council may agree to make available only to its chairman, or to all elected members of the parish council.

(c) Where a parish council wishes to make a participation allowance available to all its elected members, the allowance must be the same for all members. Only the participation allowance made available to the chairman may be greater than that paid to all other members.

(d) The independent remuneration panel for the district council in whose area the parish is located must make a recommendation about the levels of participation allowance for elected parish councillors. The district council must ensure that the parish councils in its area are aware of this recommendation. Parish councils must have regard to the recommendation when taking decisions on allowances.

(e) Parish councils will be required to publish details of the recommendation which it received from the independent remuneration panel of the district council and, at the end of each financial year, details of the participation allowances it has paid to its members.

(f) Travel and subsistence allowances will be discretionary allowances and may be paid in respect of duties specified as approved duties by the Secretary of State.

(g) Parish councils may pay elected members travel allowances for travel both inside and outside the area of the parish.

(h) Parish councils may pay elected members allowances in respect of subsistence costs incurred outside the area of the parish.

(i) Provision will be made to allow parish councils to pay a cycling allowance if they wish to do so.

(j) Where a parish council chooses to make travel and subsistence allowances available to its elected members it must have regard to the approach to these allowances agreed by the district council.

(k) Parish councils will be required to keep a record of all payments made by way of travel and subsistence allowances where these are paid. This record must specify the recipient and the amount of the allowance received. The record should be available at all reasonable time for inspection by any local government elector for the area, who may make a copy of any part of it.

Approved duties

7. It is proposed that the duties for which travel and subsistence allowances can be paid by any body should be specified by the Secretary of State – see Annex below.

Special responsibility allowance

8. Currently, special responsibility allowance may only be paid for duties specified in the Local Authority (Members' Allowances) Regulations 1991. It is minded to give consideration to extending these provisions to enable special responsibility allowance to be paid for certain quasi-judicial duties, such as service on adoption panels.

Annex – approved duties

For the purposes of the payment of travel and subsistence allowances, the following are proposed as specified "approved duties":

- a meeting of the executive;
- a meeting of a committee of the executive;

- a meeting of the authority;

- a meeting of a committee or sub-committee of the authority;

- a meeting of some other body to which the authority make appointments or nominations; or

- a meeting of a committee or sub-committee of a body to which the authority make appointments or nominations;

- a meeting which has both been authorised by the authority, a committee, or sub-committee of the authority or a joint committee of the authority and one or more other authorities, or a sub-committee of a joint committee and to which representatives of more than one political group have been invited (if the authority is divided into several political groups) or to which two or more councillors have been invited (if the authority is not divided into political groups);

- a meeting of a local authority association of which the authority is a member;

- duties undertaken on behalf of the authority in pursuance of any standing order made under section 135 of the Local Government Act 1972 requiring a member or members to be present while tender documents are opened;

- duties undertaken on behalf of the authority in connection with the discharge of any function of the authority conferred by or under any enactment and empowering or requiring the authority to inspect or authorise the inspection of premises;

- duties undertaken on behalf of the authority in connection with arrangements made by the authority for the attendance of pupils at a school approved for the purpose of section 342 of the Education Act 1996;

- carrying out any other duty approved by the body, or any duty of a class so approved, for the purpose of, or in connection with, the discharge of the functions of the body, or of any of its committees or sub-committees.

(2) SUMMARY OF PROPOSALS IN WHITE PAPER *STRONG LOCAL LEADERSHIP; QUALITY PUBLIC SERVICES*

Principal councils

A framework for high-quality public services

Building on best value and local Public Service Agreements (PSAs), a national framework will be put in place to help councils deliver better services for their communities including:

- clear priorities and exacting standards, agreed with local government;

- comprehensive performance assessments for all councils – for the first time, councils will be classified as *high-performing, striving, coasting* and *poor-performing;*

- clear and concise public information about councils' performance, including a "scorecard" available to the public so they can see how well their council is performing;

- targeted support and inspection resources according to councils' strengths, weaknesses and needs;

- extra freedoms, over and above universal deregulation, for high-performing councils that can use them to make a real difference for their communities;

- local PSAs to deliver accelerated improvements in priority services supported by additional freedoms;

- a streamlined and reformed best value framework to help councils manage improvement across all services; and

- tough and early action to tackle failing councils or services.

Drawing together performance indicator data, inspection and audit reports and using a corporate governance assessment of each council, the Audit Commission will classify each council as:

High-performing – near the top of the performance spectrum, with high performance in priority services, no poorly performing services and with proven capacity to improve;

Striving – not necessarily at the top of the performance spectrum but with proven capacity to improve;

Coasting – not at the top of the performance spectrum and with limited or no proven capacity to improve; or

Poor-performing – consistently near the bottom of the performance spectrum with limited or no capacity to improve.

High performing councils will receive extra freedoms to lead the way to further service improvements including:

- reducing revenue ring-fencing – except in respect of grants which have to be passed to schools;

- reducing ring-fencing of support for capital investment;

- ending the use of the reserve powers to cap council tax increases;

- more freedom to use income from fines;

- further reductions in plan requirements from government;

- freedom to trade more widely across the range of their services;

- more discretion over their best value review programmes; and

- a much lighter touch inspection regime.

Further freedoms will be available to *striving* councils, including access to a package approaching that available to high-performers.

Coasting and *poor-performing* councils will have their performance monitored against the action plan agreed after their comprehensive performance assessment.

Where a council is failing with little or no prospect of improvement, we will apply early intervention measures. Which measures are used will depend on the specific circumstances of the authority and the nature of the failure. They could include:

- transferring functions to other providers;

- placing the council into administration; and

- giving stronger councils (or other public bodies) a role in running failing councils.

All councils will be expected to address the extent to which greater diversity of service provision would improve performance. We will consider urgently the recommendations of the review of best value on ways in which a level playing field can be established for local government services.

Deregulation for all councils

Councils will be given more opportunity to innovate and to respond in ways that are appropriate to local circumstances by removing unnecessary burdens for all councils, including:

- abolishing the Council Tax Benefit Subsidy Limitation Scheme;

- providing greater freedom for all councils to decide council tax discounts and exemptions (subject to the results of the current consultation exercise);

- restricting ring-fencing to cases which are genuine high

priorities for government and where we cannot achieve our policy goal by specifying outcome targets;

- making councils themselves responsible for deciding how much they can prudently borrow;

- providing greater freedom for councils to invest;

- significantly reducing the numbers of plans and strategies that government requires councils to produce – we will cut the 66 plans that councils are currently required to produce by around one-third – and our target is for an ultimate reduction of at least 50% following a joint review of remaining plans with the LGA;

- scaling back on area-based initiatives and giving local strategic partnerships greater scope to rationalise partnerships;

- removing unnecessary red tape and bureaucracy including many requirements for councils to have government's consent before acting – 52 consent regime powers will be repealed and decisions on a further 30 will be taken shortly;

- providing councils with wider powers to provide services to others and to work in partnership;

- allowing councils to charge for the discretionary services they provide.

Effective mechanisms will be put in place to prevent the imposition of unnecessary new burdens.

Enhancing local democracy and community leadership

To help councils succeed as community leaders the government will:

- allow councils to introduce Business Improvement Districts, where businesses want them, to promote partnership with local businesses;

- encourage other local public sector partners to work effectively with councils, other local organisations and communities themselves to tackle local problems and exploit local opportunities;

- provide councils with more powers to serve their communities, including reviewing the range of regulatory powers currently available, for example to tackle social nuisances;

- promote further community engagement; and

- enhance democratic legitimacy and sound governance by implementing and building on the reforms in the Local Government Act 2000.

Local councils

The main proposals are:

- to legislate to increase the ceiling on expenditure under section 137 of the LGA 1972 from £3.50 per elector per year to £5 per elector per year (as in Wales), and to raise it annually in line with inflation;

- to issue good practice guidance to promote the avoidance of double taxation;

- to make it possible for parish councillors to authorise payments by their parish councils using electronic methods;

- to improve the borrowing approval system by removing the annual fixed limit, streamlining the application process and by clarifying and advertising the criteria more widely. The present annual borrowing limit (currently £8.5m a year) will be dropped, thus enabling borrowing approval to be given on demand. The maximum amount a parish can borrow will remain at £500,000;

- to pay a grant from central government to the best value

parishes. It is envisaged that each parish will receive a standard amount of £30,000;

- to give the best value parishes a general power to charge for discretionary services.

[Note: the best value parishes are those with an annual budgeted income exceeding £500,000.]

The new audit regime proposed by the Audit Commission in its paper *A New Approach to Local Council Audit* will be launched early in 2002 in time for the 2001-02 audit round. This will provide as follows:

- parishes with either receipts or payments under £100,000 will be subject to a "basic" audit which entails much self-certification and an analytical review by the auditor based on the paperwork presented;

- parishes with receipts or payments falling between £100,000 and £500,000 will be subject to an "intermediate" audit;

- best value parishes will be subject to a full audit.

Quality local councils

The government has also issued a separate consultation paper entitled *Quality Parish and Town Councils.*

The consultation paper sets out proposals for:

- a model charter on how all principal authorities and local councils should work in partnership to deliver improved services;

- the additional benefits "quality" local councils can bring to their communities, for example delivering more services and introduce high street information points; and

- a series of tests to achieve "quality" status, such as a minimum number of meetings and an electoral mandate.